OVERCOMING THE BIAS OF AGEISM IN LONG-TERM CARE

Pub. No. 20-1975

National League for Nursing • New York

CONTENTS

PART 3: RESEARCH IN LONG-TERM CARE

Gerontological Nursing Research: 1975 to 1984 .... **121**
by Irene Burnside

APPENDIX: Study Questions **141**

FOREWORD

Social and economic forces have converged to shape new challenges that today's long-term care institutions must resolve. The increasing size of our older population—particularly those over 85 years of age—and stringent cost-containment measures that release patients sooner from acute-care institutions mean that more individuals will require long-term care now and in the future. Yet economic constraints have decreased the funding available for long-term care and threaten further reductions.

Can we continue to do more with less? This is the dilemma we face in our attempt to provide quality care for all our aging population.

Over the past several years, I have had the opportunity to work with many associations devoted to health care of the elderly, includng those affiliated with nursing homes, long-term care, home health care, and hospices. I have observed first-hand how health professionals, working together, can overcome the pressures of unlimited demands and scarce resources.

This team approach is key, for the problems we face are real and many of the solutions are just now being explored. Some of the answers may lie in the papers collected here, but they need your support to take shape and become implemented as a part of the quality care nursing provides.

Jim McCall
Director of Organizational Services
Ross Laboratories
Columbus, Ohio

PREFACE

The National League for Nursing Committee on Long-Term Care and Ross Laboratories are co-sponsoring a series of invitational conferences to address essential issues in long-term care and to plan action steps that will have an impact on the field. The first conference, "Attracting Nurses to Long-Term Care Settings Through Optimal Educational Experiences," focused on special needs in preparing, recruiting, and retaining nurses for practice in long-term care settings. It resulted in the publication of *Creating a Career Choice for Nurses: Long-Term Care* (National League for Nursing, 1983).

Working within the theme of "Overcoming the Bias of Ageism through Education, Research and Evaluation," the main objectives of the second conference were to explore the following major areas and to respond to the questions posed.

Caregivers. Many individuals who choose to work in a long-term care institution gain satisfaction and remain in practice in that setting. How do we identify and isolate characteristics of people who are positive about work in a long-term care institution setting? What draws and retains these individuals?

Nursing Intervention. Nursing must address areas of its own greatest expertise. The common problems in the care of older people reflect the core of nursing practice. In some instances, early nursing intervention can make a difference between the older individual remaining at home or requiring care in a long-term care or acute-care setting. Further, the lack of some simplistic nursing interventions will make a difference in the onset or degree of illness experienced by the elderly individual. What are the common problems and major considerations in the care of the older individual?

Research. There is a trend toward the well elderly, which should not be denied. Yet the accompanying decreased attention to the frail elderly is a concern. There is need to identify

- Clinical research applicable to the long-term care setting.
- The kinds of research that can be applied in various settings.
- The successful long-term care demonstration projects, including those that are not widely publicized.

Related Questions

1. What are the implications of high technology for long-term institutional care? Are the humanistic concerns being subsumed by high technology? What are the short- and long-term implications?

2. Who is at risk in a long-term care facility? Consider: residents, families/significant others, staff, students, faculty, volunteers.

3. How is "caring" reflected in the nursing relationships in the long-term care facility? Consider:

Nurse–resident
Nurse–family/significant
  others
Nurse–nurse
Nurse–aide

Nurse–student
Nurse–faculty
Nurse–other providers
Nurse administrator–nurse
  educator

4. What do nursing service personnel need to know about clinical practice in a long-term care institutional setting? Consider:
   - Common problems
   - Crisis prevention
   - Intervention of disruptive behaviors

5. How are students socialized into the profession? What is the impact for those who choose long-term care?

6. What are the special faculty needs?

7. What are the major curriculum considerations? What "works" in basic nursing education? What "works" in continuing education?

The papers in this publication provided the stimulus for deliberations during the conference. The study questions were framed by the Committee on Long-Term Care and were based on the presentations and deliberations.

The conference was skillfully led by Sister Michael Bernadette, MS, RN, RPT, chairperson of the Committee on Long-Term Care and Director of Special Projects and Staff Development at St. Joseph's Manor, Trumball, Connecticut. Her expert knowledge and encouragement provided the impetus for open dialogue about the hard issues in long-term care. James McCall, Director of Organizational Services, Ross Laboratories, Columbus, Ohio, was a catalyst in making the conference possible and instilling the spirit and word of commitment and making a change in long-term care. A debt of graditude is due to each of these exceptional leaders in the field.

The other participants, in addition to those represented in this volume were Sister Bernadette Baer, RN, MA, Bayley Seton House, Staten Island, New York; Sister Rose Therese Bahr, RN, PhD, FAAN, Professor of Nursing, Department of Community Health Nursing/Gerontological Nursing, Catholic University of America, Washington, D.C.; Rita K. Chow, RN, C, EdD, FAAN, USPHS Hospital, National Hansen's Disease Center, Carville, Louisiana; Barbara A. Demmerle, RN, GNP, C, New Canaan, Connecticut; Angela R. Falcone, RN, BSN, MPW, Executive Director, Long Term Care Assessment Training Center, Cornell University Medical Center, New York, New York; Sherry Kittelberger, RN, MS, Director, Medical Nutritional Nursing Services, Ross Laboratories, Columbus, Ohio; Valencia N. Prock, RN, PhD, Dean, School of Nursing, University of Wisconsin–Madison; Julie Trocchio, RN, MS, Director, Delivery of Services, American Health Care Association, Washington, D.C.; Lola Westhoff, RN, MS, Assistant Director, Long Term Care, Catholic Hospital Association, St. Louis, Missouri.

Members of the NLN Committee on Long-Term Care are Sister Bernadette Baer, Irene M. Burnside, Rita K. Chow, Aaron Lynah, Lou Anne Poppleton, and Valencia N. Prock.

The participants in this conference exceeded all the challenges put forth.

Barbara Malon, MEd, RN
Director
Nursing Service Councils and Forum Affairs
National League for Nursing

PART 1: ATTRACTING AND RETAINING NURSES IN LONG-TERM CARE

STRATEGIES FOR ATTRACTING
STAFF AND FACULTY
IN LONG-TERM CARE

MATHY DOVAL MEZEY, RN, EdD, FAAN
Director, Gerontological Nurse Clinician Program
Program Director, Robert Wood Johnson Foundation
Teaching Nursing Home Program
University of Pennsylvania School of Nursing
Philadelphia, Pennsylvania

Recent changes in health care delivery and preparation of professional providers carry significant implications for staffing and faculty involvement in long-term care. These changes have the potential to place issues of policy and reimbursement for nursing homes on the national health care agenda. More explicitly, these trends include (1) the growing complexity of nursing home patients' needs for care; (2) the realignment of the customary functions of hospitals, nursing homes, and home care agencies in reference to long-term care; (3) the increase in the variety and availability of community care options as an alternative to institutional care; (4) shifts in accountability and decision making among health care providers responsible for long-term care; and (5) the increased involvement of health professional schools in long-term care practice, education, and research. Although it is as yet unclear exactly what effects these events will have on the future of long-term care, some interesting issues have emerged that, if adequately addressed, may provide data to support and direct policy and to influence reimbursement.

3

In many ways, issues of staffing in long-term care are best solved outside the educational arena. Many problems related to attracting and retaining staff and faculty in nursing homes are resolvable only at the highest level of policy and planning. For example, redress of salary inequities would go a long way toward resolving most long-term care staffing problems. A discussion of such broad solutions, however, is outside the scope of this paper. The purpose of this paper, therefore, is to pose questions that can serve both as points of departure for future discussions and as an agenda for nurses involved in long-term care.

ATTRACTING AND RETAINING STAFF

Question 1

In developing strategies for attracting and retaining staff in long-term care settings, is there a need to differentiate among professional nurse staffing roles?

Professional nurse staffing in long-term care currently consists of three groups of providers: administrative personnel, staff nurses, and nurses with advanced clinical preparation in the care of elderly nursing home patients. *Administrative nursing personnel* in nursing homes—directors and assistant directors of nursing—have unique areas of responsibility and accountability. Their responsibilities differ significantly from those of their counterparts in acute- and home care agencies and from those of other professional nursing personnel working within the nursing home. In reality, directors of nursing constitute half of the facility's management team in most nursing homes. In conjunction with the administrator, and in rarer instances with the participation of the medical director and the director of social services, directors of nursing have 24-hour-a-day, seven-day-a-week responsibility for delivery of care as well as a major responsibility to ensure the facility's compliance with state and federal regulatory demands.

The sparseness of managerial personnel in nursing homes offers opportunities for innovative management and programming with few of the bureaucratic constraints found in larger health care institutions. However, nurse administrators find themselves in charge of institutions with few readily accessible resources for advice, counsel, or relief. Whereas nurse administrators in acute-care hospitals have access to a rich pool of managerial personnel, and home care nurse administrators share 24-hour responsibility with families and other health professionals, directors of nursing in nursing homes assume sole managerial responsibility for the bulk of health care of institutionalized patients. One might reasonably assume that individuals attracted to such managerial positions possess a unique set of personal and professional characteristics, yet little is known about what factors serve to attract or retain nurses in administrative positions in long-term care or whether there is a configuration of characteristics that fosters success in these positions.[1]

Attracting and retaining *staff nurses* in long-term care, on the other hand, pose a very different set of issues. The existing level of professional nursing in nursing homes creates an extreme problem, in that there are currently very few staff nurse positions in most nursing homes.[2] Because of the absence of on-site medical care, staff nurses are called upon to make clinical decisions for which they are ill prepared and for which they receive very few incentives, either personal, professional, or financial. Opportunities for learning and for obtaining feedback about the appropriateness of clinical decisions are rare. Moreover, in addition to assuming major responsibility for patients' health care, in almost all instances staff nurses function as head or charge nurses with equivalent responsibility for day-to-day unit management. Yet such personnel take no management courses in their professional preparation and have little or no exposure to managerial theory during their professional career.

Staff nurses, then are expected to assume two divergent and, at times, conflicting positions with inadequate preparation to master either role. Experienced staff nurses have few opportunities to improve and refine clinical or managerial skills. New graduates in staff nurse positions have even fewer opportunities to obtain supervision and validation of practice behavior at the beginning level. Because of the lack of professional colleagues, institutional opportunities for learning, clinical ladders, and tuition reimbursement, the usual incentive mechanisms that serve to attract and retain staff are nonexistent in nursing homes.[3]

Nurse practitioners, clinicians, and *clinical nurse specialists* constitute the third group of nurses in nursing homes. A relatively new phenomenon, these nurses are capable of assuming broad formal responsibility in long-term care. They can modify diet and medications, develop diagnostic treatment and monitoring schedules consistent with the client's energy

---

[1] *Professional Practice for Nurse Administrators in Long Term Care Facilities* (Kansas City, MO: American Nurses' Foundation, May 1984); and E. Shields and E. Kich, "Nursing Care in Nursing Homes," in L. Aiken, ed., *Nursing in the 1980's: Crisis, Opportunities, Challenges* (Philadelphia: J.B. Lippincott, 1982).

[2] L. Aiken, "Nursing Home Priorities for the 1980's: Hospitals and Nursing Homes," *American Journal of Nursing* (1981); M. Mezey, "Confusion in Nursing Home Residents: Implications for the Health Professions," *Geriatric Nursing,* 4 (July-August 1983); and M. Mezey, L. Lynaugh, and J. Cherry, "Teaching Nursing Homes: A Report of Joint Ventures Between Schools of Nursing and Nursing Homes," *Nursing Outlook,* 32, No. 3 (1984).

[3] Aiken, *op. cit.;* Shields and Kich, *op. cit.;* and N. Strumpf and M. Mezey, "A Developmental Approach to the Teaching of Aging," *Nursing Outlook,* 20, No. 12 (1980).

levels, execute bowel and bladder regimens, and provide a host of other services supportive of daily living, rehabilitation, and personal comfort.[4]

Nurse clinicians with advanced clinical preparation carry out a variety of roles in nursing homes. Consultation, when done at the bedside with the direct caregiver present, can serve an educational function, provide confirmation of assessments, and demonstrate data-gathering strategies. Clinicians can confirm, embellish, or refute a plan of care. When necessary, referral is prompt and specific. The speedy response, collaboration among nursing staff, and ability to take action enhances the direct provider's confidence and encourages additional decision-making responsibility. The availability of nurse practitioners/clinicians assures the presence of a provider empowered to respond to the numerous acute- and chronic-care needs of nursing home patients. Geriatric nurse practitioners and clinicians report high congruence between their preparation and actual role in nursing homes and a high level of job satisfaction.[5]

This discussion highlights the variation in roles among nurses working in long-term care settings. There is some reason, therefore, to suggest that strategies for attracting and retaining nurses in long-term care should vary depending on the role of the nurse. Although it might prove relatively easy to define incentives that would make nursing homes attractive work options for nurse practitioners, such incentives may not be readily transferable to staff nurse or nurse administrator positions. Yet, to date, we have tended to discuss the attraction and retention of nurses in long-term care as a single broad issue responsive to a single set of solutions.

Question 2

Is there a need to develop projections of the numbers and types of professional nurses that are needed in long-term care?

Whether due to the advancing age of the population in general; to the increased application of medical technology that allows people with previously fatal illnesses to survive longer; or to prospective payment, which encourages earlier discharge of patients from hospitals to long-term care institutions, there is no question that individuals residing in nursing homes are becoming increasingly ill and functionally and

---

[4] P. Gabrielle et al., "Geriatric Nurse Practitioner in the Nursing Home," unpublished ms., Pittsburgh, Pa., 1980; P. Ebersole et al., "Roles and Functions of Geriatric Nurse Practitioners in Long Term Care as Viewed by Physician, GNP, and Administrator," *American Health Care Association Journal* (March 1982); M. Henderson, "A GNP in a Retirement Community," *Geriatric Nursing* (March-April 1984); and L. LeRoy and S. Solkowitz, "The Implications of Cost-Effectiveness of Medical Techology: Case Study #16: The Costs and Effectiveness of Nurse Practitioners" (Washington, D.C.: Office of Technology Assessment, U.S. Congess, July 1981).

[5] T. Rogers, L. Metzger, and R. Bauman, "Geriatric Nurse Practitioners: How Are They Doing?" *Geriatric Nursing* (January-February 1984).

psychologically disabled.[6] There is ample evidence to suggest that the mental health needs of nursing home patients remain unassessed and untreated.[7] Similarly, irrespective of whether newly defined "semi-acute"or "super-skilled" patients are taken care of in hospital step-down units, hospital-based nursing homes, free-standing extended care facilities, or in more traditional nursing homes, they pose challenges to nursing staff to adequately address their rehabilitative and recuperative needs.[8]

In 1980, the American Nurses' Association predicted the need for 118,000 to 240,000 nurses in long-term care, an increase of between 174 percent and 466 percent.[9] These staggering figures leave unanswered many questions regarding the true scope of the potential shortage of nurses in long-term care. We have insufficient data about specific staffing needs based on current and future projections of the acuity of the case mix in nursing homes. For example, what are optimal administrative units in nursing homes? What are appropriate staffing levels for patients with varying levels of acuity? What are appropriate caseloads of patients for nurse practitioners in nursing homes? Efforts to establish priorities regarding preparation of professional nurses for long-term care are severely hampered by inadequate projections of the specific staffing needs for future nursing home patients.

Question 3

Is it better to target efforts to all potential personnel, or should some efforts be concentrated on "convinced" or "almost convinced" candidates?

As an academician responsible for ensuring that gerontological content is introduced and taught in both an undergraduate and graduate curriculum, I experience frequent episodes of frustration when my colleagues question the relevance of geriatrics to the students' overall learning experience. Despite the demographic imperative of a graying population whose presence is increasingly felt in all health care settings,

[6] Select Committee on Aging, *Every Ninth American,* Comm. Pub. No. 97-332 (Washington, D.C.: House of Representatives, Ninety-Seventh Congress, July 1982); S. J. Brody and J. Magel, "DRG: The Second Revolution in Health Care in the Elderly," paper presented at the Annual Meeting of the American Public Health Association, Dallas, Texas, November 1983; and *Technology and Aging in America* (Washington, D.C.: Office of Technology Assessment, U.S. Congress, October 1984).

[7] Strumpf and Mezey, *op. cit.;* Mary S. Harper, *National Conference on Mental Illness in Nursing Homes: An Agenda for Research* (Rockville, MD: Center for Studies of the Mental Healh of the Aging, "Care of the Mentally Ill in the Nursing Home," addendum to *National Plan for the Chronically Mentally Ill* (Washington, D.C.: National Institute of Mental Health, September 1983).

[8] Brody and Magel, *op. cit.;* and "Final Report" (Kansas City, MO: Joint American Medical Association–American Nurses' Association Task Force on Improvement of Health Care of the Aged Chronically Ill, April 1983).

[9] Aiken, "Nursing Priorities for the 1980s"; and "News Watch," *Geriatric Nursing* (November-December 1980).

resistance to teaching about aging still permeates the curriculum of most professional schools. Therefore, there is good reason to avoid what S. Bergman (in a personal communication) has called the "ghettoization" of gerontology content into elective courses and specialty programs.

Figures suggest that 95 percent of nursing students choose not to work in geriatric settings.[10] Nevertheless, there are some albeit a small number of students in both beginning and advanced programs who know either prior to or soon after entering school that they plan to work in long-term care. These students' questions and concerns should lead us to rethink whether, in our efforts to ensure that all students have some contact with gerontological content, which usually focuses on the well older adult, we are failing to adequately support and encourage already or almost convinced students during their academic stay.

Two groups of students who are most likely to choose careers in long-term care are older, more mature students and nurses currently working in long-term care settings. Anecdotal and some study data suggest that students who are older, who have previously been licensed practical nurses or aides, who have worked in nursing homes at some time prior to entering an academic nursing program, or who have had positive summer nursing home experiences early on in their education are most likely to find long-term care an attractive work option.[11]

Many students now entering nursing have acquired a previous academic degree.[12] Such students, for example, those enrolled in programs that can be completed in one calendar year, come to nursing with rich life experiences and exposure to diverse educational preparation and liberal arts backgrounds.[13] These students may also be attracted to long-term care practice.

It would be enormously helpful to have data on the number of such students who express an early interest in long-term care, to know some of their characteristics, and to assess what they would see as supportive measures during the time they are in school.

We already know that nurses currently working in nursing homes are more likely to pursue a career in long-term care.[14] While their problems in achieving academic advancement reflect a different set of issues, we

---

[10] Ebersole, *op. cit.*

[11] H. T. Brower, "Survey of Registered Nurses' Preferences to Work with Certain Age Groups." Unpublished ms. (Coral Gables, FL: University of Miami, 1981); M. Campbell, "Study of the Attitudes of Nursing Personnel Toward the Geriatric Patient," *Nursing Research,* 20, No. 2 (1971); and L.M. Gunter, "Students' Attitudes Toward Geriatric Nursing," *Nursing Outlook,* 19, No. 7 (1971).

[12] A. Slavinsky, D. Diers, and J. Dixon, "College Graduates: The Hidden Nursing Population," *Nursing and Health Care,* 4 (1983).

[13] J. Bell, S. Simmons, and J. Norris, "An Alternate Pathway to a B.S.N.," *Nurse Educator* (Winter 1983).

[14] Brower, *op. cit.*

are again hampered in devising educational programs for this group of nurses by lack of data as to which and how many nurses would pursue a baccalaureate, master's, or doctoral degree in clinical care or administration if adequate resources were available. Similarly, we know little about the educational deficiences of this potential pool of applicants or about what type of programs and resources would best suit their learning needs.

Numerous strategies may be used to encourage and sustain students' interests in long-term care. In addition to scholarship and financial help, such students may benefit by forming networks and affinity groups early on in their course of study. Materials and resources could be provided, such as profiles of existing nurse providers and of exemplary long-term care institutions—"magnet nursing homes," so to speak.[15] Such materials would offer exposure to role models and provide the armamentarium needed to respond to the frequent negative comments of peers, family, and faculty about why a "good" nuse would choose to work in nursing homes.

In summary, it seems appropriate to consider redefining our attempts to attract and retain staff by identifying several strategies, including both introduction of gerontological content for all nurses and targeting programs to meet the needs of students with identified interest in long-term care.

Question 4

Are there way to highlight the positive aspects of long-term care?

The negative components of long-term care—for example, unattractive facilities, dehumanized care, and lack of professional staff—are frequently mentioned as reasons for the lack of interest in careers in aging. There are positive aspects of long-term care, however, that may be effectively marketed to attract nurses with special interests and career goals.

In discussions of long-term care with geriatric nurse practitioner students, they consistently cite independence of practice, the ability to provide continuity of care, and the ability to influence change as positive aspects of working in long-term care settings.[16] These attitudes originated in or were reinforced by positive clinical experiences in nursing homes, in which students had the opportunity to work alongside of experienced practitioners who showed enthusiasm for long-term care practice. Similarly, newly graduated nurses who take positions in teaching nursing homes—nursing homes with a critical mass of nurses who are experts in clinical practice and administration—report as positive aspects a slower

[15] *Magnet Hospitals: Attraction and Retention of Professional Nurses* (Kansas City, MO: American Academy of Nursing, 1983).

[16] Rogers, Metzer, and Bauman, *op. cit.*

work pace; increased opportunity for reflection and learning; adequate time to refine and enhance physical assessment and technical skills; and opportunities to initiate innovative programming, such as developing patient, family, and staff groups, and consultation within the community.

One potential marketing strategy to highlight the most attractive components of long-term care is the development of clinical internships in exemplary nursing homes.[17] Such model programs would allow outstanding nursing homes to serve as training grounds for the next generation of gerontological practitioners. Internships could be targeted at new baccalaureate graduates seeking supervised and educationally enriched first job experiences. Similarly, nurse practitioners/clinicians newly graduated with a master's degree may welcome an opportunity to work with master clinicians as a means of gaining increased practice opportunities and validation of clinical skills. Moreover, because nursing homes approximate small businesses, they are ideal sites to gain an overall appreciation of total, albeit small, health care systems. Such experiences could be particularly attractive to more sophisticated nurses who envision an eventual career in management, administration, or health policy.

ATTRACTING AND RETAINING FACULTY

The problems of attracting and retaining faculty parallel to some extent the staffing issues already discussed. Until recently, we have had little systematic data regarding faculty participation in long-term care. However, the Teaching Nursing Home Program initiated in 1981 by the Robert Wood Johnson Foundation has provided some insight into factors influencing the attraction and retention of faculty interested in this area.[18]

The Robert Wood Johnson Foundation Teaching Nursing Home Program (TNHP) is an experiment in cooperation between schools of nursing and long-term care facilities in clinical care, education, and research. The five-year TNHP, co-sponsored by the American Academy of Nursing, links 11 university schools of nursing and, when appropriate, other health disciplines, in affiliations with 12 nursing homes for the purpose of pooling personnel and physical and financial resources to the mutual benefit of the institutions and society. The program provides an opportunity for university schools of nursing to establish clinicial affiliations with nursing homes. The 11 participating schools of nursing represent a full spectrum of public and private institutions. Some of them have

---

[17] I. Martinson, "Gerontology Comes of Age," *Journal of Gerontological Nursing,* 10, No. 7 (1984).

[18] Mezey, Lynaugh, and Cherry, *op. cit.;* and M. Mezey, J. Lynaugh, and L. Aiken, "The Robert Wood Johnson Teaching Nursing Home Project," in E. Schneider et al., eds., *The Teaching Nursing Home: A New Approach to Geriatric Research, Education, and Clinical Care* (Washington, D.C.: National Institute of Aging, 1985).

a long history of extensive programming in gerontological nursing and collaboration between education and service settings. For others, the TNHP is the first attempt at such an initiative. The 12 nursing homes in the project include 8 voluntary nonprofit nursing homes, 2 county facilities, 1 proprietary facility, and 1 Veterans Administration home. It is hoped that these nursing homes will emerge as analogues to the teaching hospital. They may thus make a major contribution to the improvement of care to elderly persons, the recruitment and retension of nursing home staff, the training of students, and the preparation of faculty.

Participating faculty have assumed a variety of roles within the affiliated nursing homes. In all sites, faculty have positions involving direct responsibility for patient care. They serve, for example, as nurse practitioners who act as primary care providers for a caseload of patients, as clinical specialists in psychiatry and adult health, as directors and assistant directors of nursing, and as directors of quality assurance. On the other hand, some faculty have more traditional roles that involve bringing groups of students to the facility for selected clinical experiences. In some instances, faculty members' contact with nursing homes is for the sole purpose of conducting research. During the first two years of the TNHP, several questions have emerged that are relevant to attracting and retaining faculty in long-term care.

Question 5

What means can be used to increase the number and quality of faculty knowledgeable about the long-term care practice environment?

One of the major issues that has emerged from the TNHP is the small number of faculty prepared in gerontology who are knowledgeable about and interested in long-term care. Among gerontological faculty, the degree of interest in and commitment to the older adult residing in the community far outweighs interest in care of nursing home patients. Similarly, although some faculty have conducted research in nursing homes, the number of clinicians with both primary care experience in nursing homes and credentials appropriate for faculty appointment are very small. Just as staff and students frequently need to justify why ''good''nurses would want to involve themselves in nursing home care, faculty with clinical interest in nursing homes must respond to similar questions, both stated and unstated, from their professional colleagues. Moreover, few nurses have worked in nursing homes, in contrast to acute-care settings, prior to entering graduate school. Therefore, most faculty gain their first clinical experience in nursing homes during or following completion of their master's degree, when concerns regarding faculty role, publications, doctoral study, and tenure compete for their attention with concerns about problems of clinical practice.

11

In some instances, nursing homes have on their staff talented and experienced clinicians and administrative nursing personnel who have much to contribute to curriculum development and student teaching. Unfortunately, these people rarely qualify for faculty positions, and they therefore have limited opportunities to contribute to the educational program in schools of nursing. Some TNHP sites have been extremely creative in enabling nursing home personnel to involve themselves in clinical and didactic teaching activities. On the other hand, the participation of nursing home personnel will remain limited as long as they are unable to meet qualifications for faculty appointment.

An obvious conclusion, based on this discussion, is the need for renewed efforts to prepare a cadre of faculty knowledgeable in the care of nursing home residents. Several strategies come to mind. Undergraduate and graduate students must have meaningful exposure to long-term care, including didactic content and clinical experiences of sufficient length and scope to acquire competency in care of the frail elderly in the nursing home. Nursing homes need to be encouraged to create positions for and hire nurses with baccalaureate and master's preparation. One promising strategy is the development of collaborative relationships between homes and schools of nursing whereby nursing personnel can be jointly recruited, hired, and funded to the benefit of both institutions. Finally, given the federal government's involvement in financing nursing home care, it would be in its best interest to invest in the preparation of qualified nursing personnel to ensure that homes are able to deliver the level of care mandated by the expenditure of public funds.

Question 6

Given the apparent differences in their mission and in the incentives governing their functioning, what strategies can be developed to identify a mutual agenda for education and practice in long-term care?

Even when schools of nursing and nursing homes have sincere interests in developing collaborative relationships that enhance education and health care delivery, certain features of both institutions create obstacles that serve to disrupt the attainment of their goals.

In contrast to teaching hospitals, exemplary nursing homes are small and are often situated in rural or suburban settings at some distance from academic units. These institutions are community resources, responsible to local boards of directors, incorporating community volunteers, and maintaining close links with local hospitals and home health agencies. Because of the unique characteristics of nursing homes, introduction of an academic nurse into the facility in some instances immediately doubles the available professional nursing staff. It therefore becomes almost impossible for nurse faculty-clinicians not to become drawn into the nursing home environment and become directly involved in patient care and staffing concerns.

When based in the nursing homes, faculty face some natural conflicts between faculty and clinical responsibilities. While teaching is significantly enhanced by assuming a clinical or administrative role in the homes, clinical and service problems, however compelling, draw time away from teaching and research activities. Furthermore, the world of the nursing home does not always "travel well" to campus settings where it is hard to interest other faculty members in the care of a 95-year-old nursing home patient whom a faculty member may be seeing on a daily basis.

Similarly, while both faculty and homes are committed to delivering quality patient care, there is a natural tension between the concerns of nursing homes and those of faculty members as how best to achieve this goal. Nursing faculty members, accustomed to working in large teaching hospitals with unlimited resources, are unused to considering the fiscal ramifications of patient care interventions and are unaccustomed to functioning within boundaries of regulartory and fiscal contraints. Nursing homes, on the other hand, see attention to documentation and concern for the fiscal ramifications of clinical decisions as their sole means for gaining sufficient reimbursement to render quality patient care. Unless each party is able to appreciate the other's concerns, faculty members' expectations may be seen as unrealistic and nursing home personnel's responses may be seen as unconcerned and uncaring.

Question 7

How does the fact that unlicensed personnel deliver most of the direct care in nursing homes influence the attraction and recruitment of faculty?

A third issue for faculty working in nursing homes is the relationship between professional and nonprofessional nursing personnel. In most nursing homes, the bulk of direct patient care is administered by nursing aides and nursing assistants, who may have had only the most rudimentary preparation prior to employment. Even in institutions where faculty members hold dual clinical and faculty appointments and have line responsibility for patient care, aides or nursing assistants are the ones charged with implementing the therapeutic plan. Yet most faculty are unused to working directly with and supervising unlicensed personnel. Moreover, when faculty become directly involved with staff eduation, inservice courses, and quality assurance programs, they are often unprepared for the degree of instability and turnover of staff that exists in nursing homes. They are therefore faced with the same frustrations as the professional nursing home personnel, and mechanisms to sustain the enthusiasm of faculty remain equally elusive.

Despite these problems, faculty do cite many positive aspects to teaching and participating in nursing homes. Nursing homes most closely parallel nurse-managed environments. Nurses manage and control the patient's time, with physcians functioning in a consultative or collaborative role. Decisions regarding patient care are rendered in a quieter and less intense atmosphere than in the acute-care setting. Patients and families can actively participate in the decision-making process. Faculty and students are able to determine the efficacy of their therapeutic strategies, as patients stay within the institutions for a sufficiently long period of time. Furthermore, because of the current level of acuity among patients, nursing homes are ideal environments for students to acquire a myriad of technical competencies without competing for the patients' time and attention.

Despite the attractive opportunities for practice, teaching, and research that nursing homes provide, the ratio of professional to nonprofessional nursing staff remains a problem in enticing faculty into long-term care settings. In some instances faculty have responded to the challenge by creating imaginative recruitment and in-service programs. But these activities are stopgap measures which are often only temporarily successful and, irrespective of success, remain unrewarded within the university structure. With the increasing acuity of the patients now being admitted to nursing homes, the issue of nonprofessional staffing is one that deserves the attention of all parties involved in assuring quality of nursing home care.

SUMMARY

Most of the questions raised in this paper about attracting and retaining staff and faculty in long-term care are not new. While we have always assumed their existence, there are now a sufficient number of schools of nursing with direct clinical, educational, and research experiences in nursing homes to confirm both the unique opportunities and the frustrations of working in long-term care institutions. It behooves us therefore to draw on our collective experiences to seek solutions to some of these problems. For if nursing to is retain the public's confidence in its commitment to quality health care, it has no choice but to address the health needs of the frailest of those in society who require long-term care.

BIBLIOGRAPHY

Brody, S. J., and N. A. Persilly. *Hospitals and the Aged—The New Old Market.* Rockville, MD: Aspen Systems Corp., 1984.

Mezey, M., and J. Lynaugh. "Imperatives for Long Term Care." Chicago, IL: American Hospital Association National Commission on Long Term Care, 1983.

Shadish, W., and R. Bootzin, "Nursing Home and Chronic Mental Patients," *Schizophrenia Bulletin,* 7 (1981).

COMMITMENT TO CLINICAL EXCELLENCE IN NURSING HOMES

PRISCILLA EBERSOLE, RN, MS
Associate Professor, Department of Nursing
San Fransicso State University
San Francisco, California

This paper discusses the development of geriatric nurse practitioners (GNPs) as primary care providers in long-term care. It also presents the results of a survey of GNPs' own impressions of factors that enhance attraction and retention of competent nurses in the field.

Eight years ago, Barbara Lee of the W. K. Kellogg Foundation and the director of the Mountain States Health Corporation recognized the possibility of producing extremely competent nurses by recruiting and educating those nurses in the field who had demonstrated a commitment to excellence in the care of the aged.[1] The goal was articulated, two projects were implemented, and the vision was realized. Two hundred and fifty geriatric nurse practitioners are now serving nursing home populations in the United States. While these are only a drop in the proverbial bucket of 23,600 nursing homes, their presence has become visible nationwide. Why are so few nurses so noticeable? I think it is because they are filling a gap in the system.

Geriatric nurse practitioners are primarily holistic nurses who have had an additional year or more of education in the normal and abnormal aspects of aging and the management of chronic diseases. They are prepared to provide comprehensive assessments (physical, psychosocial, and functional) and to monitor and manage the common acute and

---

[1] Mountain States Health Corporation, *Improving the Quality of Care in the Skilled Nursing Facility in the Rural Mountain West* (Boise, ID: W.K. Kellogg Foundation, 1979).

17

chronic health problems of the aged. They are integral members of nursing home staff, able to care for 80 to 85 percent of the health problems that occur in most resident populations. Their presence allows for immediate attention to problems before the fulmination of acute illness, markedly reducing the need for hospitalization in acute-care centers.

Geriatric nurse practitioners are considered midlevel medical managers. However, this role is important only as it fits into the total care of the individual. Older people have medical problems, but these problems are inextricably intertwined with their social, economic, psychological, and functional needs. Geriatric nurse practitioners are so effective because they are prepared to address the needs of the total person. They work closely with attending physicians; their decisions are guided by the use of mutually developed protocols, ensuring that they will not exceed their limits and will use the physician's expertise appropriately.

The geriatric nurse practitioners with whom I am familiar were working in long-term care prior to receiving their additional education, and after the training they returned to their sponsoring agency to practice as GNPs. The question remains, What initially attracted these competent nurses to long-term care? Attracting and retaining competent nurses in nursing homes has been a major impediment to the status and quality of long-term care since the industry began developing in the 1950s. (Until ten years ago, long-term care was synonymous with nursing home care, and I am primarily concerned about the recruitment and retention of nurses in nursing homes rather than in the many levels and types of health maintenance activities included in the broader perspective on long-term care.) Some background history of this industry may be useful in analyzing the problems.

HISTORY OF THE INDUSTRY

During the "baby boom" of the late 1940s and early 1950s following World War II, this became a mobile, suburban, child-oriented society. The old folks stayed at home, while their adult children, accustomed by wartime exigencies to moving about, migrated toward places with more opportunities. Most of the nursing homes of those times were small, family-owned enterprises that bore little resemblance to the semihospital "nursing homes" of today. They often were homes, in fact, primarily providing protection, comfort, and care to incapacitated elders. The technological explosion was beginning to ignite in hospitals but had not yet affected nursing homes. As late as 1965, there was little evidence of the conceptual shift from "nursing homes" to "hospital extenders."

Medicare, instituted in 1965, has become the scapegoat for numerous dilemmas in the health care system that are, in fact, extremely complex.

However, Medicare dollars initially opened the door to major changes in the character of care to aged clients. Hospitals were able to use intensive and sophisticated diagnostic techniques and life-sustaining measures never before available or affordable. This, coupled with technological advancements and demographic shifts toward an older population, meant that numbers of frail, impaired elderly people remained alive who would not have survived in the the 1950s. This is not to imply that elderly people should not be sustained by whatever means possible but merely to state that the health care system was not prepared for the repercussions of these unpredicted demographic shifts and changes in the needs of the very old.

Great numbers of elderly persons discharged from acute care were no longer suitable for the traditional nursing home, and families were unable to cope with their complex health problems. Thus emerged the long-term care industry and the changing nature and magnitude of care required in nursing homes. In addition, the impact of diagnostic related groups (DRGs) has already been felt by nursing homes across the country, which are reluctant recipients of very ill, elderly people being rapidly moved out of acute-care settings and needing sophisticated nursing care.

Between 1969 and 1980, the number of nursing and related care homes with 25 or more beds increased by 27.1 percent, with the largest increase (more than 2,500 facilities) occurring between 1969 and 1973. In 1980, 75 percent of these were operated as commercial enterprises. It has been predicted that within a decade, less than ten major corporations will control 90 percent of the nursing home care in the United States. The trend in this direction is growing annually, and 70 percent of these home are currently under the control of large corporations.[2]

By 1980, the number of residents in nursing homes had increased by more than 75 percent over the 1969 population (1.3. million persons in 1980, as compared with 760,000 in 1969). The number of full-time registered nurses in nursing and related care homes increased by 45.5 percent during the 1970s. Full-time licensed practical nurses increased by more than 50 percent. The increase did not, however, keep pace with the increase in the number of beds.[3]

THE INDUSTRY TODAY

For geriatric nursing these trends and statistics means:

1. The long-term care industry is big business, and profit is a major goal.

---

[2] Department of Health and Human Services, *Trends in Nursing and Related Care Homes and Hospitals,* DHHS Pub. No. PHS 84-1825 (Washington, D.C.: U.S. Government Printing Office, 1984).

[3] Ibid.

2. The acuity of care among nursing home patients has increased markedly in 20 years and will continue to do so.

3. Today's nursing homes are not suitable places for the semiretired nurse (or doctor) who wishes to coast on her or his laurels.

4. Nurses are the most appropriate health care providers to meld humanism, care, comfort, and management of chronic illness to the maximum advantage of aged patients.

5. Many highly qualified geriatric nurses are needed to provide long-term care.

The good news is that recent trends indicate a more adequate supply of nurses in most areas. Hospitals are using more part-time nurses to reduce the expense of benefits. Therefore, more excellent nurses are seeking positions in nursing homes and also recognizing the challenging nature of care in these settings. Gerontological research in the past 15 years has contributed a body of knowledge emphasizing the intricacies of geriatric care. In addition, national attention has been focused on improving the quality of nursing home care through ombudsmen, senior citizens' organizations, long-term care advocacy organizations, several congressional studies, and demonstration projects such as the teaching nursing homes and gerontological nurse practitioners.

A major hurdle in attracting competent nurses to nursing homes has been their lack of education in the care of older patients. An extremely competent nurse in most areas may be entirely deficient in any theoretical gerontologic knowledge. Until recently (within the last five years) one had to attend graduate school to learn specifics of geriatric care on a level comparable to that presented in every other major specialty during basic nursing education. This is still true to a large extent, and many graduate schools of nursing still provide no track in gerontological nursing theory. Many states now require some geriatric theory in basic nursing, but they vary widely in amount and adequacy. (See "Knowledge Competencies in Gerontological Nursing," by H. Terri Brower in this volume.)

One of the best possibilities for addressing this lack lies in the emergence of gerontological nurse practitioners in nursing homes. These expert nurses are educated in certificate or graduate programs specific to the care of the aged. There are presently only 30 such programs in the United States. It is clear that many more are needed, particularly if GNPs are required in nursing homes as they are expected to be.

SURVEY OF GNPs

Having been directly involved with 120 GNPs in the last three years, I took the opportunity to survey them to determine the factors that attracted them to nursing homes and the reasons they remained there. I also surveyed other GNPs that I was able to identify in various settings. From the total of 247 questionnaires mailed there was an exceptionally high 66 percent return rate. It is clear that long-term care nurses want to be heard.

Sample Characteristics

The sample comprised GNPs and a few other nurses in long-term care. The non-GNP nurses were included because they had expressed interest in responding to the survey instrument sent to the GNPs. Among the sample population, the mean number of years in nursing was 16, and the mean number of years in long-term care was 8. Regarding educational background, 15 percent of the sample had no degree, and 83 percent were certified or had some degree. Two percent did not respond.

Their primary practice settings included 16 percent in home health care, 4 percent in life care communities, 1 percent in day care, 54 percent in nursing homes, 4 percent in clinics, and 21 percent in other settings. Among the other settings noted most often were acute-care hospitals, universities, and geropsychiatric units. Major nursing responsibilities included 54 percent in primary care management, 18 percent in consultation, 14 percent serving as director of nursing services, 4 percent serving as team leader, and 10 percent with other responsibilities.

The questionnaire asked respondents to rank in order of importance the factors they felt were most significant in answering the following questions:

1. What factors attracted you to work in long-term care?

2. What factors keep you satisfied with long-term care?

3. What are the major deterrents to attracting clinically competent nurses to long-term care?

4. What could be done to attract more nurses who are clinically competent?

Each question had at least nine possible choices (see Figure 1). The data analysis considers the five factors ranked most important by each respondent in each category, so it will not reflect 100 percent of the responses.

Attraction to Long-Term Care

The first question was "What factors attracted you to work in long-term care?" The following are the factors that were ranked most significant, along with the age of respondents that so ranked them:

Figure 1. Survey Form

Position Title:_____

Education: Dip, AD, BS, MS, Ph.D., GNP, ANP, FNP, Other____

Number of Years in Nursing_____ Number of Years in Long-Term Care*:_____

Primary Work Setting (Home Health, Hospice, Life Care, Day Care, Skilled Nursing Facility, Intermediate Care Facility, Residential, Clinic, Other [Please Specify]:

_____

What is your major responsibility?
- ☐ Primary care management
- ☐ Consultation
- ☐ Director of nurses
- ☐ Team leader
- ☐ Other: _____

Please rank responses in order of importance (1 = Most Important)

1. What factors attracted you to work in long-term care?
- ☐ Hours/flexibility
- ☐ Education preparation or experiences
- ☐ Positive experience with aged persons
- ☐ Long-term care relationships
- ☐ Care versus cure orientation
- ☐ Pay rate
- ☐ Position authority
- ☐ Role model or mentor
- ☐ Other: _____

Comments:

_____

_____

*Long-Term Care as we are using it refers to care to the aged provided for lengthy periods in institutional or community settings.

2. What factors keep you satisfied with long-term care?
   - ☐ Recognition
   - ☐ Authority
   - ☐ Primary care responsibility
   - ☐ Appreciation from patients
   - ☐ Appreciation from families
   - ☐ Appreciation of families
   - ☐ Camaraderie of staff
   - ☐ Pleasant setting
   - ☐ Benefits (specify: _____)
   - ☐ Professional opportunities (specify: _____)
   - ☐ Rate of pay
   - ☐ Hours
   - ☐ Educational opportunities
   - ☐ Other: _____

Comments:

3. What are the major deterrents to attracting clinically competent nurses to long-term care?
   - ☐ Lack of geriatric expertise
   - ☐ Peers holding negative image
   - ☐ Nonresponsive educational system
   - ☐ Negative educational experiences
   - ☐ Lack of money
   - ☐ Lack of equipment
   - ☐ Lack of interprofessional assistance
   - ☐ Lack of interest in the old
   - ☐ Lack of challenge
   - ☐ Lack of appropriate staffing
   - ☐ Public image of long-term care
   - ☐ Other: _____

Comments:

4. What could be done to attract more nurses who are clinically competent?
   - ☐ More geriatric education in basic nursing program
   - ☐ Flexible educational programs providing the working nurse opportunity for professional advancement
   - ☐ Clinical experience in nursing homes during basic education
   - ☐ Better salaries
   - ☐ Better benefits
   - ☐ Faculty interested in geriatrics
   - ☐ Advertising
   - ☐ Increased interaction between nurses in long-term care and acute care settings
   - ☐ Others: _____

Comments:

35%—Positive experience with aged persons
15%—Educational preparation or experiences
15%—Flexibility of hours
15%—Care verus cure orientation

The factors ranked second in importance were:

30%—Positive experience with aged persons
21%—Long-term care relationships
16%—Care versus cure orientation
13%—Educational preparation or experience

The factors ranked third were:

22%—Positive experience with aged persons
19%—Care versus cure orientation
16%—Long-term care relationships
13%—Educational preparation or experience

The factors ranked fourth were:

18%—Long-term care relationships
16%—Care versus cure orientation
16%—Role model or mentor
13%—Educational preparation or experiences

The factors ranked fifth were:

19%—Positive experiences with aged persons
18%—Position authority
16%—Flexibility of hours
14%—Educational preparation or experiences

The choice of "educational preparation or experiences" must be interpreted in light of the fact that most of the respondents were GNPs. The factor that seemed of least importance, rarely generating a response, was rate of pay. A cursory analysis of the responses shows that having positive experiences with aged persons attracts nurses to long-term care; and long-term care relationships and a care rather than cure orientation were consistently seen as attractive factors. We might conclude from these data that nurses attracted to long-term care are more person- than procedure-oriented and that salary is not an important motivator. Respondents' comments on this question included: "Can rise to leadership position faster than in acute care," and "Easier to practice nursing where there are few or no physicians."

Satisfaction in Role

The second question addressed was "What factors keep you satisfied with long-term care?" The following items were seen as most important by the percentage of respondents indicated:

45%—Primary care responsibility
21%—Appreciation from patients

Factors ranked second in importance were:

38%—Appreciation from patients
13%—Primary care responsibility
11%—Appreciation from families

Factors ranked third in importance were:

28%—Appreciation from families
15%—Appreciation from patients
14%—Appreciation of families

Factors ranked fourth in importance were:

18%—Appreciation of families
18%—Camaraderie of staff
13%—Appreciation from families

Factors ranked fifth in importance were:

15%—Recognition
15%—Authority
13%—Pleasant setting

Among the 14 items in this data set, factors such as hours, benefits, and educational opportunities were rarely significant in maintaining the nurses' satisfaction in long-term care. These data may not accurately reflect the desire for educational opportunities, as most of the respondents had the opportunity to become GNPs. Appreciation from families and patients and primary responsibility for patient management were most frequently cited as providing satisfaction for the long-term care nurses. Again, in this question, it appears that interpersonal relationships and job satisfaction are closely related. Comments related to the satisfaction question included: "self-satisfaction," "a job well done," "serving and advocating for long-term patients," "small interventions make a big difference to the patient."

Deterrents to Nurses

Question 3 asked, "What are the major deterrents to attracting clinically competent nurses to long-term care?" The factor ranked first in importance included:

28%—Peers holding negative image
23%—Negative public image of long-term care

16%—Lack of money
11%—Lack of geriatric expertise
8%—Lack of interest in the old

All these factors reflect the general ageism of society that permeates the professions as well as the public.

Ranked second in importance were the following items:

29%—Peers holding negative image
20%—Negative public image
14%—Lack of appropriate staffing
11%—Negative educational experiences
8%—Lack of geriatric expertise

Thus, at least 22 percent felt inadequate expertise or negative educational experiences discouraged competent nurses from seeking positions in long-term care. This, in addition to the 29 percent reporting that peers hold a negative image of the field, raises the question of whether these factors originate in the nursing education system. Remember, these nurses, who are in the field, report having very positive experiences with aged persons.

The factors ranked third in order of importance were:

16%—Nonresponsive educational system
16%—Lack of interest in the old
15%—Public image of long-term care
14%—Peers holding negative image
11%—Lack of geriatric expertise

Ranked fourth order of importance were:

19%—Negative educational experiences
15%—Lack of geriatric expertise
11%—Lack of interest in the old
9%—Public image of long-term care
8%—Nonresponsive educational system

Ranked fifth in importance were:

14%—Nonresponsive educational experiences
13%—Lack of geriatric expertise
13%—Lack of money
11%—Lack of interprofessional assistance
11%—Lack of interest in the old

Negative educational experiences or lack of them were consistently cited as third, fourth, and fifth in importance as a major impediment to the attraction of clinically competent nurses to long-term care. Moreover, "lack of geriatric expertise" appeared consistently in all five rankings. These responses indicate that the educational system must seriously examine the type and quality of geriatric experience.

Of the ten items listed, lack of equipment and lack of challenge seemed insignificant as deterrents. Although low salaries were cited only at first and fifth level of importance—and then only by an overall average of 14 percent of respondents—the issue of salary was mentioned frequently in the comments. Other comments regarding deterrents to attracting competent nurses to long-term care included:

> Nurses and others not familiar with long-term care do not see it as a challenge.

> State surveyors and bureaucrats hinder rather than help the long-term care nurse.

One respondent noted that nursing students need to be exposed to well elderly people in community settings. This suggestion corresponds with the findings of Tate, who studied 116 senior nursing students and 47 faculty from three baccalaureate schools in Colorado and Wyoming.[4] She found that senior nursing students and faculty have little interest in working with the aged, particularly in nursing homes. Students with prior work experience in nursing homes have greater interest in working there upon graduation. In the experience of the Kellogg project, recruiting the nursing home nurse and providing opportunity for advanced education has resulted in a strong commitment to long-term care. Generally, working with the aged in the community is more attractive to students and faculty.

Attracting Nurses

The fourth and last question asked, "What could be done to attract more nurses who are clinically competent?" The nurses felt the following suggestions were most important:

> 38%—More geriatric education in basic nursing programs
> 30%—Better salaries
> 14%—Faculty interested in geriatrics

The following items were judged second in importance:

> 20%—Clinical experience in nursing home during basic education
> 20%—Better benefits
> 18%—Faculty interested in geriatrics
> 14%—More geriatric education in basic nursing programs

---

[4] Juanita Tate, "Student Nurses' Attitudes Toward Work with Aged." Unpublished Ph.D. dissertation, University of Denver, Denver, Colorado, June 1984.

27

Third in order of importance were the following items:

21%—Increased interaction between nurses in long-term care and acute-care settings.
18%—More geriatric education in basic nursing programs
16%—Clinical experience in nursing homes during basic education.

Ranked fourth in order of importance were the following:

16%—Better salaries
15%—Clinical experience in nursing homes during basic education
14%—Faculty interested in geriatrics
14%—Increased interaction between nurses in long-term care and acute-care settings

Fifth in order of importance were:

14%—Flexible educational programs providing working nurses opportunity for professional advancement
13%—Better benefits
13%—Increased interaction between long-term care and acute-care nurses

The item judged least significant was advertising. Taken in its most literal sense it was not seen as useful, although a strong, positive media campaign might be helpful. It seems the real solution lies in providing a more comprehensive educational base taught by interested faculty. Twelve of the 17 ranked responses reflect these priorities.

This question produced many enlightening comments:

Educated, interested and involved faculty are needed to teach geriatrics in basic programs.

There have to be improvements in $$$ to attract good, competent nurses to long-term care.

Raise salaries so they are competitive.

I believe nurses involved in long-term care have a different personal and philosophical perspective of nursing than other professionals.

Clinical experience with well and ill elderly needed during basic education programs.

Our societal values are at the heart of the dilemma in attracting more people in long-term care.

Support of student experiences would promote positive interchange.

Better pay is still the top drawing card along with better working conditions, particularly in nursing homes.

Better salaries, because less pay is often connotated to mean "not as good a nurse."

It begins with the basic nursing education, but the stereotype of the nurse in the "nursing homes" must be changed.

Although doing some of these things is expensive, I feel that a campaign, etc., would be the quickest and simplest way to educate a larger section of the population.

Need more emphasis on compassionate care at all levels of nursing education and practice. We need to be reminded often that nursing exists to serve the interests of the patient; that the patient is our reason for being in nursing.

Stress ambulatory care, home health care in care of aged. Students turned off by hopelessly regressed patients could be turned on by strong copers and survivors in community.

In all my years in educational preparation, few faculty could "stand" geriatrics. Those very few who really were interested were real catalysts for me.

Nursing home experiences are usually at the beginning of a nurse's education—often creating unpleasant experiences (mainly due to lack of expertise, etc., but unfortunately students remember the experience as being poor due to the geriatric setting). I would like geriatric experiences to be available to students later in their education, when they feel more comfortable in their role and are then able to fairly evaluate geriatric settings.

Nursing Home vs. Other Settings

Because community long-term care might engender significantly different responses from caregivers than nursing home experience, the data accumulated were subjected to bivariate comparison of nursing home nurses versus the non-nursing home nurses. Fifty-four percent of the nurses were in institutional settings (skilled nursing facilities, intermediate care facilities, residential), and the remaining 46 percent worked in various other capacities.

The following differences emerged in the nurses' major responsibilities:

Responsibility	Nursing Home	Non-Nursing Home
Primary care management	23%	31%
Consultation	11%	7%
Director of nursing services	11%	3%
Team leader	3%	1%
Other	6%	4%

The nursing home and other settings appear to provide nearly equal opportunities for autonomy, decision making, and independent action.

In response to the question of what factors attracted them to work in long-term care, the following differences were noted: 10 percent more nursing home nurses were attracted because of positive experience with aged persons; 9 percent more nursing home nurses liked the long-term care relationships; and 10 percent more non-nursing home nurses sought the care-versus-cure orientation.

In their comments regarding Question 1, nursing home nurses mentioned such factors as "temperamentally suited to position"; "leadership positions accessible"; "easier to practice nursing where there are no doctors convenient." Nurses based in other settings commented: "possibility for creativity and variety"; "new role"; "wanted to advocate for old"; "challenging, time to provide holistic care."

On the second question, regarding satisfaction in the setting, 35 percent more non-nursing home nurses stayed because of primary care responsibility, and 10 percent more because of appreciation from patients. In their comments regarding this question, nursing home nurses mentioned "recognition"; and "creative approaches to health care possibile"; and "personal maturity has brought desire to serve." Non-nursing home nurses stressed "variety in work load"; "autonomy"; "challenging"; "requires creativity"; "continual learning and patient progress is satisfying."

Regarding deterrents in recruitment, 15 percent more nursing home nurses felt inadequate salary was a factor. Thirteen percent more nursing home nurses thought peers' negative image of long-term care was a deterrent, and 12 percent more thought public image was significant.

In their comments on Question 3, nursing home nurses suggested: "Boredom and frustration causes nurses to leave"; "peers think there is little challenge"; "frustration with bureaucrats, policies, surveyors, paperwork"; and "requires personal willingness to become involved." Nurses in other settings commented: "Education doesn't provide exposure to well elderly"; and "noncompetitive salaries, poor staffing, patients depressing, helpless, dependent."

In response to the fourth question, 12 percent more nursing home nurses thought better benefits would attract more competent nurses; 5 percent more mentioned better salaries. Among the non-nursing home nurses, 18 percent more suggested faculty interested in geriatrics would help. Nursing home nurses' comments on this item included: "better salaries"; "educated, interested, and involved faculty"; "positive media image"; and "long-term care nurses have a distinctive personal and philosophic perspective." The non-nursing home nurses wrote: "Education clinical experiences with full spectrum of elderly"; "nursing and medical management must provide more than lip service"; and "better salaries."

Differences in nurses' perceptions depending on educational background were also analyzed through bivariate comparision. (See Table 1.)

Table 1. Differences in Responses to Survey by Education

Question	Without Degree	With Degree
1. Attraction to long-term care	20% more noted hours/flexibility Only 1 noted educational preparation 15% more noted long-term care relationships	17% more noted educational preparation
2. Satisfaction in role	20% more noted appreciation from patients 16% more noted appreciation from families 14% more noted appreciation of families	
3. Deterrents to nurses	30% more noted inadequate salary 13% more noted lack of appropriate staffing	20% more noted lack of geriatric expertise 18% more noted public image of long-term care
4. What could be done to attract competent nurses	20% more noted better salaries 30% more noted experience in nursing homes during basic education	33% more noted faculty interest in geriatrics

Nonranked Data

Some nurses in the survey did not rank order data but checked all the responses they considered important. These data were analyzed separately. The check-marked data set included 51 respondents. While these responses were not ranked, numerical predominance of responses clearly indicated the important factors. Factors that attracted this group to work in long-term care included:

- Educational preparation or experiences
- Positive experience with aged
- Long-term care relationships
- Care versus cure orientation

Factors that contributed to satisfaction in long-term care were:

- Primary care responsibility
- Appreciation from families
- Appreciation from patients

The major deterrents to attracting competent nurses to long-term care were:

- Peers holding negative image
- Lack of geriatric expertise
- Negative educational experiences
- Lack of money
- Public image of long-term care

To recruit more competent nurses, the following factors were judged most important:

- More geriatric education in basic nursing programs
- Better salaries and benefits
- Clinical expertise in nursing home during basic education

CONCLUSION

This survey was biased by the preponderance of GNPs who reacted from a position of influence and specialization. Nevertheless, the major initiatives needed to attract and retain clinically competent nurses seem to lie in structuring positive experiences with aged persons early in the educational experience; increasing geriatric expertise and thus awareness of the complexity and challenge of gerontological care; promoting positive images of gerontology among peers and combattng ageism in general; and, finally, making nurses aware of the opportunities and demands in the field. Before these changes can occur, faculty must recognize the remnants of their outdated experience in caring for the aged that have influenced them in less than positive ways. When faculty members recognize their lack of geriatric expertise as one source of their discomfort with the subject and when they are provided realistic opportunities to attain proficiency, they will generally respond. Of course, the issue of salary will always recur, but as gerontological care becomes increasingly complex and the supply of proficient nurses inadequate, salaries are beginning to reflect the market demands. The long-term care field is responsive to image and fiscal profit. Those who are innovative in the industry recognize that proficient care accomplishes both their major goals and are eagerly seeking well-qualified gerontological nurses. It is up to nursing education to provide them.

The field of gerontological nursing has opened the door to upgrading the status of the entire nursing profession. The aged need more nursing care than any other segment of the population. Nurses who are realistic will seek the opportunties and become the standard bearers for the twenty-first century. The job of nurse educators is to prepare them and demonstrate the opportunities.

BIBLIOGRAPHY

American Academy of Nursing. *Primary Care by Nurses: Sphere of Responsibility and Accountability.* Kansas City, MO: AAM, 1979.

American Nurses' Association. *Guidelines for Appointment of Nurses for Individual Practice Privileges in Health Care Organizations.* Kansas City, MO: ANA, 1978.

_____.*Guidelines for Short-Term Continuing Education Programs: Preparing the Geriatric Nurse Practitioner.* Kansas City, MO: ANA, 1974.

_____.*The Primary Health Care Nurse Practitioner.* Kansas City, MO: ANA, 1980.

_____.*Standards of Gerontological Nursing Practice.* Kansas City, MO: ANA, 1976.

Bates, Barbara. "Physician and Nurse Practitioner: Conflict and Reward." *Annals of Internal Medicine* (May 1975), pp. 702–706.

Brody, Stanley, et al. "Geriatric Nurse Practitioner: A New Medical Resource in the Skilled Nursing Home," *Journal of Chronic Diseases* (August 1976), pp. 537–543.

Brown, Kathleen. "Nature and Scope of Services Joint Practice," *Journal of Nursing Administration* (December 1978), pp. 13–15.

Brown, Martha M. "The Need for Reallocation of Health Resources," *Nursing Homes* (January-February 1980), pp. 12–15.

Edmonds, Marilyn. "Responsibility Charting," *Nurse Practitioner.* (January-February 1981), pp. 39–41.

Fruend, Cynthia, and George Overstreet. "The Economic Potential of Nurse Practitioners," *Nurse Practitioner* (March-April 1981), p. 28.

Gerdes, John, and Sidney Pratt. "In Anticipation of the Geriatric Nurse Practitioner," *Nurse Practitioner* (November-Dember 1978), p. 14.

Grimaldi, Paul, and Toni Sullivan. "Medicaid Reimbursement of Long Term Nursing Care," *Geriatric Nursing* (March-April 1981), pp. 133–138.

Little, Marilyn. "Physicians' Attitudes Toward Employment of Nurse Practitioner," *Nurse Practitioner* (July-August 1978), pp. 27–30.

Lowenthal, Gilbert, and Robert Breitenbucher. "The Geriatric Nurse Practitioner's Value in a Nursing Home," *Geriatrics* (November 1975), pp. 87–91.

National Joint Practice Commission. "Joint Practice in Primary Care: Definition and Guidelines." Chicago: NJCP, 1977.

————. "Position Statement on the Education of Nurse Practitioners. New York: NLN, October 1979.

National League for Nursing. "Position Statement on Long-Term Care." New York: NLN, February 1984.

Romm, Joseph, et al. "The Physician Extender Reimbursement Experiment," *Journal of Ambulatory Care Management* (May 1979), pp. 1–12.

Sullivan, Judith, and Judith Warner. "Economic Perspectives for Nurse Utilization of the Nurse Practitioner," *American Journal of Public Health* (November 1978), pp. 1099–1103.

Trandel-Karenchuck, Darlene, and Keith Trandel-Karenchuck. "State Nursing Laws," *Nurse Practitioner* (November-December 1980), pp. 39–41.

Weisberger, Edward. "The Nurse Practitioner: Medical-Legal Considerations," *Scalpel and Quill* (June 1976).

Weston, Jerry. "Distribution of Nurse Practitioners and Physician Assistants: Implications of Legal Constraints and Reimbursement." *Public Health Reports* (May-June 1980), pp. 253–258.

ATTITUDES TOWARD THE ELDERLY: NURSING STUDENTS' PERSPECTIVES

AARON LYNAH
Former Board Member
Nursing Student Association of New York State
New York, New York

During my early years as a nursing student, my attitude toward working with the elderly was perhaps typical of most young people. I was under the impression that all senior citizens were confined to nursing homes, senile, and completely dependent upon others for activities of daily living support. One of my first jobs in a health care setting, a ward clerk on a general medical-surgical unit, did little to encourage a positive attitude toward working with the elderly. When I revealed that I was a nursing student, many of the nursing staff were eager to supply various bits of helpful information and, with the clients' permission, occasionally allowed me to observe various nursing procedures.

It was exciting at first, but as time elapsed I grew tired of the experience. I began to wonder if nursing was for me. As I inquired deeper into my own thoughts, I realized that it was not the thought of being a nurse that disturbed me as much as the thought of working with "old people." Most of the clients admitted to our unit were elderly. Many of them had moderate to severe and sometimes terminal health condi-

35

tions. At best, it was a terribly frightening experience. I listened as countless men and women cried out for a multitude of reasons. They all seemed so helpless.

Overheard conversations among the medical and nursing staff created mental images that did little to induce an interest in working with the elderly. Occasionally, family members would visit for brief moments. Often they would make comments suggesting that these elderly individuals were predominantly responsible for their ill health. Overall, it was a depressing situation. I was of the opinion that I did not wish to work with "old people," but I believed that my bias had some sort of rationale. I often felt that gerontology was not interesting enough. I wanted something more exciting and intellectually challenging. It seemed certain that gerontology could not offer this.

During some of my earliest clinical rounds I found it difficult to interact with elderly clients. Most of them reminded me of the patients I encountered as a ward clerk. I began to feel guilty because I did not fully understand why I maintained this bias toward the elderly. My attitude began to change during the beginning of my junior year in nursing school. I became involved in various extracurricular activities in nursing, such as the National Student Nurses Association. Through my participation in this organization, I met with numerous nursing students of various backgrounds and interests. We shared a great many positive aspirations for nursing. A significant number of my colleagues expressed a sincere interest in gerontological nursing. Some were certain that gerontological nursing would be their specialty. The majority, however, maintained interest in other areas.

At this time, many of the nursing lectures at my school concentrated on gerontological nursing. A number of our instructors strongly encouraged us to seriously consider gerontological nursing as a specialty. They made it seem exciting as they spoke of the numerous opportunities and challenges of this field. I remained somewhat skeptical, although curious, and uncertain of which specialty in nursing would suit me best.

It was not until my clinical rotations in the community that my bias toward the elderly began to show any signs of modification. During these experiences, I began to view the elderly as independent, functioning citizens. Excitement was ever present. This area of nursing appeared to present great promise in terms of intellectual and professional development. My only disappointment was that these clinical rotations were too short. I began to seriously believe that working in the field of gerontology offered some hope.

Months later, much to my surprise and delight, I was asked to act as the representative from the Nursing Student Association of New York State to the National League for Nursing Committee on Long-Term Care. My participation on this committee was met with great enthusiasm. The opportunity to exchange ideas and opinions with leading educators in nursing provided an even greater incentive toward specializing in gerontology.

My experience on the committee led me to wonder whether significant numbers of nursing students maintained any serious interest in gerontological nursing. To this end, a survey was distributed at the National Student Nurses Association convention in Oklahoma City in April 1984. (See Table 1.)

The purpose of this survey was to gain an understanding of the type of course content and experience students were exposed to as well as their actual clinical experiences. It should be pointed out that this survey was exploratory in nature, and the results are limited by the lack of respondents (116 students responded) and the number of questions answered by respondents.

Although it is not practical to draw conclusions based on information collected in this survey, it does raise serious questions concerning the manner in which students are socialized into gerontological nursing. It appears that the greater majority of students would not prefer this specialty. Until significant changes or modifications in our institutions and in society are made, however, much of the current bias toward the elderly will remain, thus decreasing the potential number of professional nurses qualified to practice in the field of gerontological nursing.

Table 1. Survey of Nursing Students

Question	Response (percentage)
1. Age	
18–20	18
21–30	51
31–40	28
41–50	3
2. Type of program	
Associate	18
Baccalaureate	62
Diploma	20
3. Sex	
Male	3
Female	97
4. Ethnic/cultural background	
Black	2
Hispanic	4
Oriental	2
Caucasian	91
5. Is gerontology incuded as a subject in your curriculum?	
Yes	88
No	12
6. If you answered yes, is the subject:	
One or more courses?	12
Part of another course?	19
Integrated into the curriculum?	52
A required course?	14
7. Is long-term care nursing included in the nursing curricuum in your school?	
Yes	92
No	7
Do not know	1
8. If you answered Yes to question 7, is long-term care:	
A combination of theory and structured clinical experience?	93
In theory only?	3
A structured clinical experience only?	4

Question	Response (percentage)
9. When do you obtain long-term care nursing experience?	
First clinical experience	51
Senior	26
Other (specify) (most common response was "work as an LPN")	23
10. Do you have an opportunity to work with all of the following: Physical therapists, occupational therapists, recreational therapists, social workers, activities directors?	
Yes	85
No	15
11. Is long-term care provided as an elective?	
Yes	11
No	81
Do not know	8
12. If long-term care is not included in the curriculum, do you think it should be?	
Yes	86
No	3
Do not know	11
13. If you had a long-term care or gerontology course, would you choose this type of setting to work after graduation?	
Definitely	4
Possibly	53
Never	24
Do not know	19
14. Is there a faculty member at your school with:	
a. Advanced training in long-term care?	
Yes	56
No	16
Do not know	28
b. Gerontological nursing?	
Yes	56
No	12
Do not know	30
15. If you answered Yes to question 14, has this person been available as a resource to you?	
Yes	97
No	3

Table 1, continued

Question	Response (percentage)
16. Does your clinical experience include:	
Discharge planning	18
Community experience	20
In-patient clinical rotation	19
Skilled nursing facility	25
Health related facility	16
Other	2
17. How much time does your school devote to teaching long-term care?	
One semester	30
One quarter	29
One year	18
Other (most common response was "during entire time in nursing school")	23
18. Does your curriculum include a course or courses on death and dying?	
Yes	68
No	32
19. In what area of nursing specialty do you plan to practice?	
Long-term care	2
Gerontology	4
Medical-surgical	29
ICU/CCU/ER	24
Operating Room	5
Anesthesia	3
Community health	15
Other (pediatrics and midwifery were most common)	27
20. Optional question: What types of personal experiences have you had in your life with elderly people or people with long-term illnesses? (33 out of 116 respondents—28% answered.)	
Cared for elderly friend or relative	24
Worked as an LPN or as an aide in hospital or nursing home	76

ENVIRONMENTAL INFLUENCES THAT AFFECT NURSING STAFF

LOU ANNE POPPLETON, MS
Director, Home Health Services
Meridan Healthcare Corporation
Towson, Maryland
and
MELANIE COX, RN, MS
Nursing Consultant
Meridan Nursing Center
Towson, Maryland

The environmental influences that work to either attract and retain or repel and lose staff in a nursing home have three distinct characteristics. These are (1) the physical and structural aspects of the environment, (2) the organizational or managerial aspects of the environment, and (3) the social factors that influence care. Each has its impact on how staff relate to patients, other staff, and the tasks of the environment as well as on the staff's sense of fulfilled purpose or professional and personal well-being.

Several disturbing statements found in the literature clarify why patients, families, and even professional staff have an active or residual fear of becoming involved with long-term care services in these most valuable medical and human service facilities. It is an underlying uneasiness that they will be co-opted into some form of misappropriated or misused power. Consider the following statements:

Unlike prisons and mental hospitals, special settings for the aging do not change people deliberately, except to facilitate their care. Nevertheless, there is growing concern that their very organization may induce learned helplessness with apathy, regression and despair masked as "inevitable" organic impairment. . . .

The institution's central feature is its all encompassing nature. All of the activities of daily living take place in this single setting under the direction of the same authority. Thus the nursing home bed can be viewed as the final resource and its withdrawal, the ultimate threat.

The environment has the power. The only resources the patient has are his or her own remaining abilities.

Controlling the patients' resources of mobility and facilities for defecation further lowers the patients' bargaining power.[1]

Clearly, the statements are troubling. They remind us of the overwhelming possibilities for misuse of power in the nursing home environment. These possibilities, as well as the perceptions of these possibilities, are among the strongest reasons why urgent and pressing interdisciplinary professional interest in long-term care facilities and services must continue.

Nursing homes are the fastest-growing health care facilities in the United States.[2] The demographics tell us why. The rapid growth of the elderly population will continue well into the next century, and the fastest-growing group are those 85 or older. In 1982, 2.4 million Americans were 85 years of age, an increase of 9.1 percent over the previous two years. Of those individuals, 32,000 were over age 100. While this age group consitutes less than 1 percent of the population now, they fill more than 20 percent of the beds in nursing homes. By the year 2000, 5.1 million people will be at least 85, and by the year 2030, 8.8 million adults, almost 33 percent of the population over 65, will be 85 years of age or older.[3]

It is this group, the frail elderly, those over 80 years of age, who need the most help in balancing the real and perceived powers inherent in the nursing home environment. It is primarily this group, with their unique problems of diminishing capacities, coupled with their needs for love, protection, and skilled professional services, to whom we must ad-

---

[1] Mary Gwynne Schmidt, "Exchange and Power in Special Settings for the Aged," *International Journal for Aging and Human Development,* 14, No. 3 (1981-82), pp. 157–175.

[2] Barbara Heller et al., "Nurses' Perceptions," *Journal of Gerontological Nursing,* 10, No. 7 (1984), pp. 23–25.

[3] Bureau of the Census, "America in Transition: An Aging Society," *Current Population Reports,* Series P-23, No. 128 (Washington, D.C.: U.S. Department of Commerce, December 1983), pp. 3–5.

dress our current and future activities in order to attract and retain competent staff.

We must become sensitive to ways of opening opportunities for professional fulfillment *and* professional recognition, both within the nursing home milieu and in the external professional community. We must develop ways of balancing the actual or perceived power that is represented in both the physical plant and the organizational and managerial practices of the administrative, supervisory, and caregiving staff.

THE PHYSICAL PLANT

"What you see is what you get." This oft-repeated phrase describes the common reality of a nursing home's physical environment. The state of the art in the construction of new facilities is quite different from what was known or applied when the many older or converted buildings in which a large number of nursing home patients now reside were constructed. While most facilities comply with the regulatory standards that are established by state statute, these are usually minimum standards. Much can be done in even the smallest or cut-up environment to make the physical plant more homey and livable for both patients and staff.

First and foremost (after fire and safety standards) would be cleanliness and odor control of the kitchen, the floors, the beds, and the furniture. There are known ways to combat these problems—simple ways that need only the good will and direction of the administrative and supervisory staff to identify the problems and work toward resolution on a day-by-24-hour-day basis. This step alone would be tangible evidence that the environment was under control. It would demonstrate that the power of administrative and supervisory sensitivities was directed toward, at a minimum, keeping the environment clean, safe, odor free, and a pleasant place to live, work, and visit.

A second set of miscellaneous factors that should be attended to include bright, restful colors on walls and floors and at the windows; good lighting; the use of plants, music, and pets; bulletin boards creatively managed to communicate visual, colorful, and useful information; a bustling yet calm sense of movement and activity; and soft, caring voices and personal attention to residents. All these tangible and intangible factors would again demonstrate that the power to manipulate the physical environment was being used as a positive and creative energy on behalf of all who live, work, and visit there.

Third, and perhaps most important, a professional and caring staff must have adequate supplies available to them to meet the patients' care and comfort needs and to effectively complete the medical care plans. Nothing can be more consistently disruptive than to have to "beg, borrow, or steal" the linen, treatment supplies, medications, or personal care items essential for patient care. Professionals or paraprofessionals who have any pride in their capacities to provide needed services will not long put up with such artificial restrictions, poor planning, or power-motivated economies in the physical environment. A nursing home or nursing center is just that—a physical place, a temporary or permanent home where people reside, not because they want to, but because they *need* nursing care. Therefore, the physical plant or environment has as its only task the perpetuation of a stable, organized, supportive, and responsible space in which the best form of individualized and aggregate nursing care can occur. Supplies are needed for service. It is that simple.

OTHER STRUCTURAL INFLUENCES

To broaden the discussion, other structural areas must be explored as well. Staffing, the type and number of residents, and reimbursement all become major environmental influences. For example, the type and proportion of staff are as important as the total number. In 1980, 23,000 nursing homes provided care for 1.4 million residents and employed approximately 700,000 nursing personnel, three-quarters of whom were nursing assistants. Registered nurses constituted 12 percent of nursing personnel. Of the 41.8 full-time equivalent nursing personnel for each 100 residents, the ratios of registered and licensed practical nurses were 4.5 and 5.5 respectively. In skilled nursing homes, registered nurses' care was provided for an aggregate of 12 minutes in a 24-hour period, compared to 2.5 hours for the average hospital patient. In the facility classified as intermediate, 7 minutes of registered nurses' care was provided. Nursing assistants provided six times as much nursing care as did registered nurses and five times as much as licensed practical nurses.[4]

The impact of these statistics on recruitment and retention of nurses is threefold. The first subliminal message is this: If the expectations of nursing care in long-term care facilities can be met by this high percentage of nonprofessional staff, then registered nurses' time and expertise would be wasted. Second, there is neither time nor availability of skilled personnel to work to change the status quo. There are no extra layers of people who can join forces to do research or, even on an informal basis, utilize the nursing process to do effective problem solving. A third, positive aspect of this lack of layers is the close proximity of the direct care providers to top nursing management. Testimony at sessions of the Maryland Commission on Nursing Issues revealed that nurses viewed

[4] "Nursing Personnel," *Report to the President and the Congress on the Status of Health Personnel in the United States*, Vol. 1, Part C (Washington, D.C.: U.S. Department of Health and Human Services, Division of Nursing, August 1984), p. C-1-33.

the layers and hierarchy in hospitals to be detrimental to nursing.[5] This problem does not exist in most nursing centers. We need to build on this advantage and identify ways of using it to its maximum potential to promote staff motivation.

Many nurses say they resist long-term care because they are not involved in giving direct patient care. They see themselves as doing paperwork or managing a unit. Again, this is a negative that can be turned into a strong positive one. As direct caregivers, nurses potential influence on care is limited to the residents and families we work with. This is a limited number of people on any given day. However, by working through others, we can increase our influence to include the total unit. We need to recruit the type of nurse who sees the professional role as a teacher and a motivator and who enjoys working through others to accomplish larger tasks that benefit larger numbers of people.

Linked closely to staffing is reimbursement. Cost consciousness, which is just now affecting hospitals with the advent of prospective payment and same-payer legislation, has dominated long-term care for years. Only 3 percent of residents in long-term care facilities are covered under Medicare or other private third-party payers. Approximately 55 percent are covered by Medicaid, with the remaining 42 percent paying privately.[6]

Our purpose is not to pursue the nuances of reimbursement, but surely it is evident from these figures that there are limits on the costs that can be rolled over into private payment fees if the nursing home is to remain competitive in the marketplace. In addition, Medicaid and Medicare have caps that have been very effective in controlling long-term care costs. Nursing administration must become creative in designing patterns of nursing utilization that render quality care that is cost-effective. This must be viewed as one goal, not two.

While each long-term care facility has its own personality in terms of residents, we are beginning to see a shift in some facilities to the sicker resident. This is a result of several factors. First, the nursing home population is getting older and residents are staying in facilities for a longer period of time, with their various needs becoming more complex as their capacities diminish. A second factor is the impact of prospective payment on hospitals. This is evidenced in newer facilities and cetain other centers rather than industrywide at this time. As we have more experience under prospective payment, its impact on the acuity of residents' problems should become more global. This increased acuity might be expected to have a positive ripple effect on recruitment and retention. Time will tell, but there is also the possibility that it will have a negative ef-

---

[5] "Executive Summary," *Report of the Governor's Commission on Nursing Issues*, Vol. 1 (Annapolis: State of Maryland, August 1982), p. 5.

[6] "Facts in Brief on Long Term Health Care" (Washington, D.C.: American Health Care Association, 1984), pp. 18–19.

fect. The philosophy of nursing intervention toward achievement of goals is different in long-term care than in acute care. Nursing is just at the point of identifying the unique body of knowledge for gerontology. There is still a long, hard battle to be fought if we truly are going to meet the needs of our aging population. We cannot simply plug in a "high-tech skills" mentality into our environment and assume that nurses are going to be challenged. The influence of this high-tech movement away from the holistic, humanistic philosophy of long-term care is going to be a powerful force to resist.

The unique body of knowledge that we need in gerontological nursing—or rather, the lack if it—deserves attention. How many of us know what the norms are for physical assessment for a 75-year-old black female? How do you do a mental status assessment? What are appropriate interventions for a 68-year-old male with Alzheimer's disease who walks incessantly? What is the normal blood sugar for an 82-year-old woman? Where do you go for these answers? These are questions our long-term care nurses are faced with every day with no answers. No wonder they are frustrated or feel their work is unimportant! Fortunately, this dearth of information is being recognized and slowly being corrected, but research, publication, and general public acceptance will take time.

ORGANIZATION AND MANAGEMENT

One of the major functions of management is to help individuals examine what they think and do, day by day, and to roughly assess the impact of their attitudes and behaviors on others. Another major function is to take one or two steps up the ladder of abstraction to look at the broader decisions that have a major, long-range impact on the organization and its performance.

Organizations, like people, are always evolving. In fact one can understand a lot about organizational behavior with good grasp on the subtleties of human behavior. As anyone will attest who has spent time there, nursing homes on any given day portray the entire range and drama of human behavior. Thus, managment must manipulate the functions of the organization (a creative use of power) to control chaos, to protect those who need protection, to motivate those who need motivation, and so on.

The key question is: How do you organize and manage the environment, through the power of manipulation, so that everyone—patients, staff, families, and administrators—all win? or receive positive rewards? or receive fulfillment in their jobs? or feel good about their experiences? Clearly, these questions must be considered on the ladder of abstraction mentioned earlier.

One author's thesis suggests that a nursing home is filled with individuals, patients, staff, and family who have unresolved conflicts about their participation in the environment. Therefore, any characteristics of the environment that reinforce or contribute to the unresolved conflict will have a negative impact on the individuals' motivation and sense of well-being. Gordon identified individuals who work in nursing homes as having the following characteristics.[7] They:

1. are service oriented, committed to doing good and helping others as a goal that is valued in itself.

2. want fair wages and decent working conditions.

3. find that helping others is a self-validating experience.

4. are relationship motivated, like to work in groups, and enjoy each other.

5. need a great deal of recognition. Since very old patients are often unable to assess the technical qualities of their care and may be unresponsive, preoccupied, or uncooperative, the recognition must come from others, preferably supervisory and management staff.

6. like team work and interdependence.

7. enjoy dependable and predictible approaches to change.

8. have a sense of emerging professionalism and want to identify with professional values and learn new skills of new applications of old skills.

9. have conflicts about working in nursing homes because they must defend their vocational choice to the outside world. They have problems accepting low staffing ratios. They also have difficulty understanding their own sense (fear) of aging and some families' responses to the resident and their problems.

Gordon further suggested that the factors that motivate employees to overcome or work through their conflicts, thus allowing them to continue their employment, are those organizational and managerial functions that decrease their anxiety and offer them the rewards that meet their previously listed needs. The most important factor, in his judgment, is a competent, mature administrator who totally believes that the personnel in the organization are its most important resource.

Other important organizational factors are the following:

---

[7] George Kenneth Gordon, "Developing a Motivating Environment," *Journal of Nursing Administration* (December 1982), pp. 11–16.

1. Having a thoughtful and organized recruitment and selection process.

2. Developing stable and predictable work group assignments that are varied with cause, planning, and explanation whenever possible.

3. Sponsoring supervisory training as an ongoing activity in the environment, utilizing good supervision as a power to release workers' potential for creative work experiences.

4. Timely and frequent recognition for efficient and effective work activities.

5. Encouraging staff and patients to be creative—to suggest, plan, and implement systematic change, allowing opportunties to be spontaneous without disruption.

This view of an active, participatory, interactive environment is one in which some areas of "power" are appropriately shared with the workers and recipients of services. This view is promoted by Hiatt, an environmental psychologist-gerontologist.[8] She believes that the use of space and the arrangement of the physical and social environment influences therapeutic possibilities, the capacity for self-reliance, and mental competency. She states that both staff and the public alter their perceptions of older individuals based on expectations associated with the setting. Conversely, it is the responsibility of staff to use their creative powers to manipulate the environment, to motivate creativity, and to reinforce problem-solving and self-reliance skills that positively influence perceptions of older adults. She questions whether factors in the environment contribute to agitation, incontinence, wandering, calling out, throwing food, spitting, or aggression. Could these be attention-getting behaviors, which could be altered or influenced by social and other human contact changes in the environment? If we understood more completely how to constructively manipulate these antisocial behaviors, would it decrease the stress on the residents and the staff and thus help to promote staff retention?

Other positive suggestions for staff and environmental development that might foster "binding" to the environment are the following:

1. Shifting the focus of people who care for "things" in the environment to program concerns, thus offering all staff a cross-departmental view and creating support for each others' tasks, responsibilities, and employment needs.

---

[8] Lorraine G. Hiatt, "The Environment as a Participant in Health Care," *Journal of Long-Term Care Administration* (Spring 1982), pp. 1–15.

2. Greater involvement with the community; developing support or self-help groups to engage in mutual activities such as public relations and positive expressions of the value and credibility of professional services within the institution.

3. Developing an emphasis on rehabilitation within the institution that conveys the message of caring while stretching for attainment of positive goals.

Another factor that has been mentioned in the literature as having a positive impact on environmental stimulation and intellectual growth for nursing home staff has been the development of ongoing and active clinically oriented in-service education programs. If it is to compete with other employers for quality-oriented, competent staff, management must engage and solve the problem of meeting employees' perceived needs for more knowledge and skills in a way that promotes their learning objectives while accommodating staffing on all three shifts.

As Myers and Myers state:

> Employees desire a supportive and informative feed-back network within the long-term care facility. The most common employee frustrations are often the result of their not knowing what is expected of them, how they can improve what they are doing and why are they doing it.[9]

They also stressed the premise that employees are a facility's most important asset, and assets must be carefully managed and developed. In-service education is an excellent forum in which to reduce frustration and increase cohesiveness, credibility, and accountability within the institutional environment. Its capacity to help retain staff can be directly attributed to cost-effective measures with positive budget implications.

THE SOCIAL MILIEU AND ITS IMPACT

Society's view of aging is reflected in the attitudes of the professional community toward gerontology and long-term care nursing. The paucity of graduate programs in gerontology, the lack of courses in gerontology in basic nursing programs or medical schools, and the lack of clinical experience in nursing centers perpetuate these attitudes. Fortunately, this is also beginning to change. Ways of fostering these changes must be pursued by the industry. Perhaps we must work to be included in collegial relationships within schools of nursing, to establish scholarships

---

[9] Paula Myers and Roger Myers, "In-Service Education: A Model For Success," *Journal of Long-Term Care Administration* (Summer 1984), pp. 24–26.

for study in this area, to support certification programs in gerontology, and to provide fieldwork for research. Probably the most important influence, however, would be for those of us who are engaged in long-term care to be proud of what we do. It can be a self-fulfilling prophecy. If we are proud of what we are, other will be also.

Nursing in a long-term care institution requires an emotional involvement with and commitment to residents, families, and staff. This degree of involvement results in a highly stressful job and requires an outlet or professional support system. As mentioned earlier, the size of many facilities dictates the need for small numbers of licensed staff—often fewer than 20. Few people are therefore available to form the needed support systems to help each other. If administration recognizes this need, again, creative solutions can be identified. One company has developed "quality circles," based on the Japanese system, consisting of all levels of staff on a unit. Staff learn to help and support each other, regardless of their previous background or credentials. Although there are no definitive data available at this time, preliminary results are positive enough to expand the program into additional facilities.

Lack of support from a professional perspective also contributes to nurses' frustrations in long-term care facilities. A nurse in this environment is responsible for assessments and decisions about residents' health status. Many nurses have not been prepared to make these judgments, nor are there other nurses who can be called upon to verify an assessment or decision. Many nurses cannot cope with this awesome responsibility. Although this has not been identified as a problem by nurses, surely it is a reason they are continually citing a need for educational programs. Again, the question is how to provide this support without falling back on the traditional supervisor's approach utilized in the past by hospitals. Is this the place for a geriatric nurse practitioner? Options must be identified. If the present support system remains the same as residents become sicker, frustration and turnover can only increase.

SURVEY OF NURSING HOME EMPLOYEES

A recent attitudinal survey of the staffs of 11 nursing centers in Maryland, administered in 1982 and again in 1984, gives some clues as to how staff likes and dislikes in their environment might affect retention, job satisfaction, and skills development.[10] Important characteristics identified by the study were the following:

- Is the workload equitable and reasonable?
- Are disciplinary actions fairly applied?

---

[10] "Meridian Healthcare Corporate Attitude Survey." Unpublished study (Baltimore, MD: Meridian Healthcare Corporation, July 1984).

- Do they receive adequate information about what is going on?
- Does the firm "care" about them?
- Is there cooperation between departments?
- Is there adequate linen? Supplies?
- Is the laundry adequate?
- Are their accomplishments recognized by supervisors and administrators?
- Do they feel part of the management team?
- Are they comfortable in being able to express concerns to the director of nursing and the administrator?
- Are there opportunities for growth?
- Are salaries and benefits equitable between institutions?
- Is there cooperation between nursing and social services?
- Is there enough staff to meet patients' needs?
- Does management really support nursing?
- Are the personnel policies clearly stated and accessible?

SUMMARY

We have attempted to identify some of the physical, structural, organizational-managerial, and social aspects of the environment that influence ways of attracting and retaining staff in long-term care institutions. Although far from complete in offering anectodal suggestions or documented approaches, this discussion suggests that individuals interested in this problem must understand that developing specific, positive approaches is a "power-full" approach to a seemingly "power-less" problem.

PART 2:
CORE CONTENT
IN LONG-TERM CARE

KNOWLEDGE COMPETENCIES IN GERONTOLOGICAL NURSING

H. TERRI BROWER, Ed.D, FAAN
Professor, School of Nursing
University of Miami
Coral Gables, Florida

The work of the National League for Nursing's first invitational conference on Attracting Nurses to Long-Term Care through Optimal Educational Experiences laid important groundwork for the second conference.[1] The first conference raised a substantial number of important issues concerning gerontological nursing curricula. Some of the particular concerns raised were the necessity for faculty and students to clarify values regarding attitudes and issues of quality of life, as well as the necessity for careful inclusion and structuring of the nursing home experience in the curricula for all undergraduate students.

Clarification of values becomes even more essential as we move into an information-processing type of society. Cost accountability in acute-care hospitals has been virtually absent in the past as costs escalated beyond all projections and hospitals vied with one another to obtain the most advanced technological equipment. The arrival of diagnostic related groups (DRGs) for costing for health care has caused outcries of concern that quality of care will suffer in the end. As the population continues to age, we find older people requiring more intensive services, staying longer, and suffering more complications in hospitals than younger persons. Now, with the advent of DRGs aimed at curbing Medicare costs, older patients are being discharged after progressively shorter hospitalizations to the nursing home or directly to the community. For many older individuals, these earlier discharges are resulting in greater acuity of

---

[1] National League for Nursing, *Creating a Career Choice for Nurses: Long-Term Care* (New York: NLN, 1983).

illness upon discharge than in the pre-DRG era. Health care costs are shifting, as is the need for service delivery. Indeed, the shift to out-of-hospital care is so pronounced that federal funding for long-term care is expected to double from $2.6 billion in 1984 to more than 4 billion for 1988.[2] The need for expert gerontological nursing care at home, in the hospital, and in the nursing home will continue to grow.

Long-term care presents many challenges to nursing education because it comprises many options, entry points, and types of supportive health and social services for functionally impaired persons. Unfortunately, for too many nursing faculty members, long-term care continues to be synonymous only with nursing homes and does not reflect the entire array of institutional and community-based services.

NURSING AND LONG-TERM CARE

Long-term care is continually being redefined. The following definition has been adapted from the National Association of Area Agencies on Aging:

> Long term care viewed from the perspective of a continuum provides a broad array of services offering a range of preventive, maintenance, and acute episodic health and social services for older persons who have a self-care deficit. Services may be community based, in the home, or institutional settings and are geared towards the most cost effective and least restrictive environment. An effective long term care system has case management as the central component and depends on service integration and coordination, appropriate client assessment, maximal use of informal supports, and ongoing evaluation.[3]

While nurses work in a great many of the service settings, many settings have no nurses on staff. For optimal utilization of services, however, nurses must be knowledgeable about how the system functions as well as how to get access to the services that are available. Since health and social assessment, locating, coordinating, and monitoring services, including periodic reevaluation, are all central components of client management in long-term care, one could conjecture that nurses should be the case managers. If nurses served as case managers, they would be more intimately aware of the type of services available to meet the changing needs of older clients. Unfortunately, for much of the country, social workers and others have filled and continue to fill the role of case managers, although they are not able to provide appropriate health assess-

---

[2] S. Sternberg, "Medicare Revisions May Mean Shortcuts in Care," *Miami Herald,* August 7, 1984, p. 7A

[3] P. Otazo, "Overview of Long Term Care." Report prepared for the Planning and Special Projects Committee (Miami, FL: Area Agency on Aging, May 14, 1984), p. 4.

ment. Perhaps nurses are not filling case managerial roles because they lack significant input into strategic policymaking groups where the role of case managers is defined.

THE AT-RISK POPULATION

Long-term care services are directed primarily to the "at-risk" population—so designated because of their frailty and requirements for supportive services. This is a group of older persons with which nurses frequently come in contact, either for maintenance or for acute episodic care. When gaps in service are found, there is a greater tendency to institutionalize members of this group. Although less than 5 percent of the aged are currently in nursing homes, the older one gets, the greater the likelihood of entering a nursing home. The at-risk group is largely comprised of "old old" persons. The number of this group—those over age 85—has been greatly underestimated. The 1967 population projections for 1980 were underestimated by 10 percent for all persons over age 65, compared to the actual 1980 census, but projections for those over age 85 were underestimated by more than 25 percent. Similarly, only 1.4 percent of those between 50 and 74 are in nursing homes, while 22 percent of those over 85 years of age are found in nursing homes.[4] The proportion of the "young old" will continue to decrease, as the 75 and older age group continues to expand until the end of the twentieth century. Whereas the proportion of those age 75 and older was only 4.4 percent in 1980, this figure is expected to be 5.5 percent by 1990 and 9.8 percent by 2030. It is clear that the "old old" portion of the at-risk population will continue to grow in the future.[5]

Although the aging of the population is most often defined chronologically, it is essential that other definitions of aging be included when describing the at-risk group. Determinants such as sociological, behavioral, psychological, and functional aging can assist in differentiating among aging populations and individuals. In addition to the risk factor of advanced age for requiring nursing home or increased home-based services, dependency in activities of daily living and physical or mental disorders rank highest as correlates of the population served in nursing homes. Older people in colder climates are almost twice as likely to reside in a nursing home, and the very old who are without a spouse are more than two dozen times as likely to be institutionalized than younger old people who are married.[6]

[4] D. L. Rabin, "The Aging of the Population and the Changing Demand for Long Term Care." Paper presented at the Annual Meeting of the American Geriatrics Society, Denver, Colorado, May 15-18, 1984, p. 2.

[5] E. Chelimsky, *Medicaid and Nursing Home Care: Cost Increases and the Need for Services are Creating Problems for the States and the Elderly* (Washington, D.C.: U.S. General Accounting Office, May 1983).

[6] W. Weisert and W. Scanlon, *Determinants of Institutionalization of the Aged* (rev. ed.; Washington, D.C.: Urban Institute, July 1983), p. 12.

The U.S. Public Health Service has estimated that mortality rates can be directly related to life-style, the environment, and adequacy of the health care delivery system. Life-style alone accounts for 54 percent of deaths from heart disease, 37 percent of deaths from cancer, and 49 percent of deaths from cardiovascular health problems.[7] Thus, it is no surprise that diagnoses of mental illnesses; injuries; cancer; or digestive, blood, metabolic, genitourinary, or circulatory disorders among older people were found to be significant predictors of nursing home use. Surprisingly, those having nervous or respiratory disorders have very low rates of institutionalization.[8]

Demographics can not only assist in pinpointing those in need of services, but can also describe service utilization of older adults. For example, those over age 65 make on the average two more visits per year to a health care provider than those under 45; in 1980, those over 65 made 6.4 visits compared to 4.4 visits for those under 45. Hospital admissions are more than two times greater per year for those over 65 as for the population as a whole—354 hospital admissions per 1,000 of people age 65 compared to 160 per 1,000 admissions for the population as a whole in 1979. The length of hospital stay for the over-65 group is substantially greater than for the population as a whole; 10.6 days for those over 65, and 7.6 days for those under 65.[9]

All those over the age of 65 join the at-risk group when they are hospitalized. Nurses working in acute-care settings come in contact with two types of hospitalized older persons: those who have a transient or short-term health problem and those with an exacerbation of a long-term or chronic health problem. Nurses working in hospital settings need a strong knowledge base in gerontological nursing. They must especially be aware of community and informal support systems to deter unnecessary institutionalization and to use available support systems to the fullest. But nurses also need to be aware that support systems may be fragile. When an elderly spouse assumes too large a share of the burden of care it may result in or exacerbate an existing health problem for the spouse.[10] Estimates indicate that informal support systems provide 80 percent of health services for the frail older person in the community. When support for family care is neglected, the situation may result in *two* functionally disabled older people.

Also included in the at-risk population are older U.S. veterans who are eligible for many of the long-term care services offered by the Veterans

[7] J. S. Siegal and M. Davidson, "Demographic and Socioeconomic Aspects of Aging in the United States," *Current Population Reports* (Washington, D.C.: Bureau of the Census, U.S. Department of Commerce, 1984).

[8] Weisert and Scanlon, *op. cit.*

[9] Siegal and Davidson, *op. cit.*

[10] S. J. Brody and N. A. Persily, *Hospitals and the Aged: The New Old Market* (Rockville, MD: Aspen Systems Corp., 1984), p. 53.

Administration (VA). Veterans over age 65 are eligible for VA services, depending on service availability. Although veterans currently constitute 45 percent of all American males over the age of 20, by 1990 more than 50 percent of all U.S. males over 65 will be veterans.[11] The number of veterans over the age of 60 will double between 1980 and 1985. About 27 percent of veterans discharged from VA hospitals in 1982 were 65 or older. The average age of veterans treated in VA nursing homes was 70.1 years in 1977, much younger than the national average.[12] The demand for services for aging veterans who are suffering from chronic conditions is increasing at a startling rate. Many VA nurses are involved in developing innovative long-term care services. The rich resources of the VA should be considered when planning nursing curriculum.

NURSING EDUCATION

Most nursing faculty now agree that gerontological nursing content is necessary in undergraduate nursing programs. There is disagreement, however, about the amount of time that should be spent on theoretical content in gerontological nursing. Some faculty members consider that mere inclusion of content on physical changes in normal aging adequately addresses the need for didactic content. Even less sound is the belief of some faculty that since clinical experiences in caring for older persons are provided with older clients, there is no particular need to include didactic content in the curriculum.

Sullivan's research highlights this problem.[13] She analyzed responses of faculty and graduates from 19 midwestern nursing schools, both public and private. Respondents were asked to rate the importance, amount, and type of gerontological nursing content to be included in future BSN curricula. Gerontological nursing content was ranked less important and also received a smaller number of recommended hours of content allocation among the public schools of nursing than in the private schools of nursing. Among recent graduates of BSN programs, students ranked gerontological nursing content as greater in curricular importance and recommended more content hours be devoted to gerontological nursing than did nursing faculty.

Tollett's research, carried out in Texas, reported similar findings.[14]

[11] Special Committee on Aging, U.S. Senate, *Developments in Aging: 1983, Vol. 1* (Washington, D.C.: U.S. Government Printing Office, 1984), p. 392.

[12] Chief Medical Directors, *The Aging Veteran: Present and Future Medical Needs* (Washington, D.C.: U.S. Government Printing Office, 1978), p. 17.

[13] K. W. Sullivan, "The Importance, Amount, and Type of Gerontological Nursing Content Recommended for Future Bachelor of Science in Nursing Curricula: A Survey of the Opinions of BSN Faculty and Practicing BSN Graduates. Unpublished doctoral dissertation, Kansas State University, Manhattan, Kansas, 1984.

[14] S. M. Tollett and C. M. Anderson, "The Need for Gerontologic Content Within Nursing Curricula," *Journal of Gerontological Nursing,* 8 (1982), pp. 576–580.

Practicing nurses in her study indicated a preference for pathological content; this may have reflected an awareness of their lack of educational preparation in gerontological nursing. The large majority of Tollett's respondents believed gerontological nursing content should not be offered in the first semester of the nursing program. In spite of this belief, most programs in Texas that include gerontological nursing content primarily emphasize normal processes of aging during the first semester.

Another study by Tollett and Thornby looked at 12 baccalaureate schools of nursing to determine the total amount of time spent on gerontological nursing content.[15] They did not indicate whether *content* meant both clinical experiences and theoretical content in the curriculum; nor were specific content and faculty's qualifications for teaching gerontological nursing identified. They concluded that the amount of gerontological content in a nursing curriculum was not related to changes in students' stereotyping of older persons.

Fortunately, there are contrasting examples. When a three-year federally funded curriculum project was initiated in 1980 at the University of Miami's School of Nursing, a cognitive test in gerontological nursing was developed. Pretesting revealed that faculty had minimal knowlege in the field; the average score was about 50 percent.[16] Faculty improved significantly after the three years, indicating that with a concerted effort, faculty can learn specific theory and content in gerontological nursing.

When the University of Miami's baccalaureate curriculum was reviewed to determine what gerontological nursing content was being taught, the analysis did not identify a logic or pattern for incorporation of content; physical changes of normal aging were presented on three occasions, while little else was taught in gerontological nursing. Fifty percent of the faculty did not even know normal aging changes. In keeping with other self-report surveys, of course, self-reporting by faculty on inclusion of gerontological nursing content cannot be assumed to be accurate.

Another by-product of the University of Miami project was the opportunity to compare the knowledge of and attitudes toward aging of students in two similarly funded projects with differently structured curricula. The University of Miami's curriculum was based on a transcultural, integrated curriculum model. The other program, located at Wilkes College's Department of Nursing in Wilkes Barre, Pennsylvania, used a developmental, blocked curriculum structure. As ex-

---

[15] S. M. Tollett and J. Thornby "Geriatric and Gerontology Nursing Curricular Trends," *Journal of Nursing Education*, 21: (June 1982), pp. 16–23.

[16] H. T. Brower, "Curriculum Considerations in Baccalaureate and Graduate Education," in *The Aging Society: A Challenge for Nursing Education* (Atlanta, GA: Southern Regional Education Board, 1983), pp. 47–59.

pected, students in the blocked curriculum achieved significantly higher cognitive scores on the aging posttest than students from the integrated curriculum. Students from both programs had significantly more positive attitudes at the completion of the project than at pretesting.[17] The difference between the students' positive attitudinal change in these projects and the lack of change in attitude found by Tollett and Thornby may be attributed to the leadership of knowledgeable gerontological nursing faculty and teaching of carefully structured content.

Another finding centered around the choice of working with the elderly, which is considered an important indicator of the success of curricular structuring. It was interesting that at posttest more students in the integrated curriculum selected the response choice of working with the elderly, but at the completion of the course fewer students in the blocked curriculum stated they would choose to work with the elderly. The investigators felt that for students in the blocked curriculum, earlier exposure to nursing faculty not knowledgeable in the care of older persons had a lasting negative impact, in addition to the inappropriate use of a nursing home clinical for beginning students. Students enrolled in the integrated curriculum, in contrast, were initially exposed to enthusiastic teachers and relatively well elderly people in community settings.

A 1980 study of content inclusion in Florida's nursing schools implied that faculty in technical level programs were focusing more attention on gerontological content than those in baccalaureate programs.[18] Janelli replicated this study in New York State in 1982 and found that the majority of deans and directors, like their counterparts in Florida, felt that most of their faculty possessed sufficient expertise in gerontological nursing.[19] New York State had eight faculty members prepared in gerontological nursing compared to none in Florida. Only 2 New York programs out of 36 used a specific gerontological nursing test, as did only 3 out of 21 in Florida. The concurrence of these findings indicates that academic leaders have widespread misperceptions concerning the adequacy of faculty preparation in gerontological nursing. These studies confirm, moreover, that few faculty members have had prior experience in a nursing home.

NEED FOR FACULTY

The House Committee on Appropriations, in its fiscal year 1984 budget report, requested the Department of Health and Human Services

---

[17] H. T. Brower, A. M. Kolanowski, and R. M. Tappen, "Integration or Separation for Gerontological Nursing." Paper presented at the Tenth Anniversary Meeting of the Assocation for Gerontology in Higher Education, Indianapolis, Indiana, February 1984.

[18] H. T. Brower "Teaching Gerontological Nursing in Florida: Where Do We Stand?" *Nursing and Health Care,* 11, No. 10 (1981), pp. 543–547.

[19] L. Janelli, "Exploration Study of Gerontological Nursing Content in Undergraduate Curriculum in New York State. Unpublished MS., Niagara University, New York, 1983.

to submit a report with a plan of action to improve and expand training in geriatrics and gerontology. Sadly, in its five pages on nurses, the report somewhat glossed over educational needs. Nonetheless, among the Ad Hoc Committee on Enhancement of Training in Geriatrics and Gerontology's recommendations, several are worthy of consideration:

1. Health professional schools should have faculty with expertise in aging to conduct substantial and high quality basic graduate and continuing education programs and to serve as role models on educational content.

2. Educational programs should include both didactic and clinical experiences and should involve work with both well and ill elderly. Information on aging should be integrated throughout the curriculum whenever applicable.

3. Education and training should be of adequate duration to develop the knowledge and skills required for high quality performance.

4. Academic programs should be linked on a continuing basis with community programs including hospitals, long term care, and ambulatory services to ensure interchange of ideas and experiences.

5. The existence of negative attitudes towards the elderly should be recognized and countered by more positive and realistic attitudes and approaches. Educational programs should emphasize sensitivity to the unique health, emotional, social, cultural, ethnic, and other circumstances of older adults.[20]

The committee estimates a need for 2,000 nursing faculty with preparation in gerontological nursing to adequately staff graduate and undergraduate programs. But as of 1980, only 420 nurses—less than 1 percent of those with advanced degrees—held a master's or doctoral degree with a primary focus in geriatrics and gerontology. To thus categorize together nurses with doctoral and master's level preparation reflects the committee's lack of understanding of the structuring of advanced nursing education.

Students majoring in gerontological nursing at the master's level will find that levels of expertise upon graduation vary greatly, depending on the quality of their program. Two surveys of master's level programs found a wide variation in the curricula offered.[21] Particularly disturbing in the more recent review was the scarcity of programs that offered a course focusing on long-term care. It may be that a number of programs

---

[20] Ad Hoc Committee on Enhancement of Training in Geriatrics and Gerontology of the Department of Health and Human Services, *Report on Education and Training in Geriatrics and Gerontology* (Washington, D.C.: National Institute on Aging, 1984), p. 16.

[21] H. T. Brower, "A Study of Graduate Programs in Gerontological Nursing," *Journal of Gerontological Nursing,* 3, No. 6 (1977), pp. 40–46; and Brower, "Graduate Education in Gerontological Nursing Revisited," *Nursing and Health Care,* 5, No. 7 (1984), pp. 390–395.

are being implemented as a response to funding initiatives and less as a reflection on the program's ability to deliver available, qualified faculty prepared in gerontological nursing. Besides availability of qualified faculty, both surveys found that a major block to further expansion or conduct of current programs was difficulty in recruiting students. When nurses are not introduced to gerontological content at the undergraduate level, they do not readily perceive that there is anything to be learned concerning care for the aged at the graduate level.

It is encouraging that in spite of significant problems, master's programs in the specialty continue to expand, with new ones opening each year. There were more than 50 master's programs offering a major or minor focus in gerontological nursing by Fall 1982. The rate of growth, from 8 programs functioning in 1977, indicates that there could easily be 75 such programs by Fall 1984. A number of nurse educators and leaders are recognizing the necessity to develop specialists in gerontological nursing. These programs will greatly enhance nursing schools' ability to recruit and integrate more adequately prepared faculty into the teaching of generic students—if there is a perceived need to do so.

Doctoral preparation focuses on the need for theory construction and rearch ability with the assumption that specialist preparation has taken place at the master's level. Dye's review of 35 nursing doctoral programs for gerontological nursing preparation found heavy reliance on substantive preparation at the master's level.[22] Although five programs reported offering a "focus" in gerontological nursing, it was extremely difficult, if not impossible, to identify any particular curricular activity in gerontological nursing.

Because the doctorally prepared nurse is recognized as having the highest credentials, that person is given instant recognition as an expert in the field. Wolanin cites the uncomfortable example of a doctorally prepared nurse who has never had even one course in gerontological nursing.[23] The nurse dislikes "nursing" and would under no circumstances practice nursing care of older clients. She is teaching and "doing some research because how else can one make a living?" Yet, because of her doctoral preparation, she is in demand as a speaker and expert in gerontological nursing.

Another problem with the current cadre of doctorally prepared nurses is that most have a doctorate outside of nursing. Gerontological nursing research is desperately needed to establish credibility for the specialty. But doctorally prepared nurses most frequently conduct inquiries that are reflective of sociology, psychology, education, and the like. It would appear that most of us have not developed the level of sophistication

---

[22] C. A. Dye, "Doctoral Preparation for Gerontological Nursing." Paper presented at a symposium on The Development of Gerontological Nursing Education, at the 36th Annual Scientific Meeting of the Gerontological Society of America, San Francisco, November 1983.

[23] M. O. Wolanin, personal communication, June 21, 1984.

necessary to conduct more meaningful nursing research. However, this will begin to change in the future as more nurses who have been prepared at the master's level in gerontological nursing obtain their doctorates in nursing.

SPECIALTY RECOGNITION

The failure of academic leaders in nursing to recognize gerontological nursing as an academic and practice specialty is a major deterrence to inclusion of its content in curricula, leading to limited influence in curriculum development. If the specialty nature of gerontological nursing were recognized, there would be less of a perception that faculty have sufficient expertise even when they lack appropriate credentials such as practice experience, published research, scholarly papers, or a master's in the specialty.

Robbins, Mather, and Beck's explication of the problems engineered by a lack of specialty recognition for geriatric medicine can easily be extrapolated to gerontological nursing.[24] In addition, compounding the delayed development and status of gerontological nursing education is the lack of recognition in academia on a national level. Although geriatric medical educators have had several funded national forums on geriatric education, beginning in 1976, there have been no similar forums for gerontological nursing educators. As Robbins, Mather, and Beck point out, geriatric/gerontological societies, as multidisciplinary organizations, have not responded to the unique issues of specialty credibility.

The problem of specialty recognition is further complicated by the sparseness of nurse gerontologists, resulting in too little research productivity. In addition to nursing groups, gerontological nurses belong primarily to two multidisciplinary groups: the American Geriatric Society (AGS) and the Gerontological Society of America (GSA). The AGS is a physician-oriented group. Nurses rarely present papers at AGS meetings and even more seldom have manuscripts accepted for publication in their official journal. Nurses belong to various sections in the GSA, since they do not have their own section, with a majority belonging to the Clinical Medicine Section. However, nursing is recognized as one of the specialties within the Clinical Medicine Section. The GSA has two official publications, *The Gerontologist* and the *Journal of Gerontology*. Nurses are rarely published in *The Gerontologist*. The *Journal of Gerontology* publishes research emanating from the various sections of the GSA, with space allocated according to the number of sections. Nurses may occasionally have a book review published or appear as third or fourth of many authors in the Clinical Medicine or Biological Sciences Sections of the journal. Although greater numbers of nurses than any

[24] A. Robbins, J. Mather, and M. Beck, "Status of Geriatric Medicine in the United States," *Journal of the American Geriatric Society*, 30, No. 3 (1982), pp. 211–218.

other profession spend time working with older clients, fewer nurse have reached a level of parity with other members of the gerontological scientific community. Therefore, even if gerontological nurses had their own section, in the organization, it is doubtful that they would be capable of producing sufficient research compared to other sections in the GSA.

In spite of the low numbers and level of professional development, nurse gerontologists are responding to the need to increase their scientific stature. An increasing number of nurses and nurse faculty are presenting research papers at the GSA and the American Association of Gerontology in Higher Education. Unfortunately, not only do gerontological nurses have limited power and influence in these societies, but there is also scarce representation from the academic nursing power structure. In effect, scholarly gerontological nurses speak mainly in forums with others who have mutual concerns. While, it may be comforting to commune with others who face similar conflicts and problems, this strategy results in circular activity and contributes to the myth that there is limited research activity in gerontological nursing. Adding to the myth are several overall reviews of nursing research that report exceptionally limited research in gerontological nursing.[25] However, the reviews were performed by nurses who are not gerontologists, and the publishing sources nurse gerontologists use most heavily, particularly the *Journal of Gerontological Nursing*, were not included. Such reporting perpetuates the misconception that, if there is limited research activity, there must be little to teach in gerontological nursing. Nurse gerontologists must begin to speak in greater numbers before nursing societies and to publish in the more recognized journals oriented toward nursing research to obtain recognition as a specialty.

CONTENT AND CURRICULUM ISSUES

The categorizing of amount or type of content for various levels of professional development begins to emerge when issues of breadth versus depth are discussed. Baccalaureate education, the first level of preparation for entry into professional nursing practice, continues to be faced with ever-burgeoning demands for more additions. These demands are reflected in the resistance of faculty to the adding of gerontological nursing content and contributes to the feeling that there is no more room in the curriculum without significantly revising what is currently there. Although this ongoing conflict will never be completely resolved, it is time to raise ideas about substantive changes in structuring basic baccalaureate curriculum. Change is essential to provide a more adequate

---

[25] P. H. Brown, C. A. Tanner, and V. P. Padrick, "Nursing's Search for Scientific Knowledge," *Nursing Research,* 16 (1984), pp. 26-32; and K. A. O'Connell, and M. Duffey, "Research in Nursing Practice: It Present Scope, in N. L. Chaska, ed., *Images of Nursing: Views Through the Mist* (New York: McGraw-Hill Book Co., 1978).

match between preparation in expected graduate competencies and the real practice world.

Consideration of who is served and how well prepared graduates are to serve older clients leads to the realization that several highly specialized services such as pediatrics and maternal and infant care are not offered in many hospitals, rarely in home health care, and seldom in a nursing home. Although these two specialty areas require significant time in theory and clinical practice in a basic program, only a small percentage of nurses will ever work in one of these areas after graduation. These specialty areas could be designated specialization areas to be taught only at the postbaccalaureate level. Such curriculum restructuring would have the advantage of providing adequate time for the content that is specific to the clients most graduates will work with.

With the primary focus of undergraduate preparation being at the generalist level, specialty preparation at the master's level, and research preparation at the doctoral level, a position statement could be developed covering the scope and detail of content to include at each level. However, at this stage of development, with basic programs varying from inclusion of almost no content beyond normal physical changes to a highly sophisticated gerontological emphasis in the curriculum, one cannot be sure where specialization content should be initiated at the master's level. Likewise, most current doctoral students who focus on an area of aging research will not have had specialist preparation at the master's level. Although doctorally prepared graduates will have been schooled in the rigors of nursing theory development, research design, methods, and analysis, many will be unprepared for the faculty roles needed by schools of nursing to provide the necessary gerontological curriculum input.

Most courses taught at the doctoral level are in research methodology, theory development, and the like, conducted in a seminar format. They intentionally build on the level of expertise obtained at the master's level. Master's preparation builds on the base of knowledge obtained at the baccalaureate level. Content categorization can guide curricular engineers in designing curricula which ensure that certain spheres of knowledge are included. Each school of nursing has a unique curriculum, a unique organizing framework. Because of the muddled state of the art in gerontological nursing education, with few entering master's students having had basic content and many of those graduating with a doctorate having had little content, a leveling of knowledge areas can direct the selection of core content. Although specific content may not be taught in a doctoral program, peers can expect a person possessing a doctorate to have acquired knowledge in substantive gerontological areas. These areas would of necessity be in greater breadth and depth. Certainly, the knowledge included should cover many more areas than the master's level of preparation. Moreover, areas of knowledge expected to be covered can be more easily molded to each program's conceptual and structural model. Ferrario stresses that essential content based on practice models might be more useful to guide developing programs.[26]

IDENTIFYING NECESSARY KNOWLEDGE COMPETENCIES

To begin to identify the knowledge competencies expected at each level of education, a study was carried out using a conceptual framework developed earlier.[27] Gerontological content was organized under the four major areas of Normative Aging, Pathological Aging, Nursing, and Policy Issues. Twenty-four experts in gerontological nursing education were asked to critique and rate areas of knowledge that nurses should have on a Likert scale consisting of: unnecesary (1), perhaps (2), if possible (3), should be included (4), and essential (5). Respondents were requested to provide ratings for undergraduate, master's, and doctoral levels and to add or delete knowledge areas as they believed necessary.

Fourteen of the experts responded, for a response rate of 58%, and several wrote letters with their specific input and concerns. Computations were completed for only 13 of the respondents because one survey was returned late. Some respondents stated that, at the least, topics need to be introduced at the baccalaureate level and receive increasing depth of knowledge at other levels. A number had difficulty responding to the question of what knowledge competencies doctoral students should have and wrote in comments such as "should have by now." At the same time, they gave these areas low ratings, indicating that they may have interpreted the task as ranking for content inclusion instead of for knowledge competency, as stated. Checking with one respondent by phone confirmed that was the case.

Most respondents did not rate the knowledge levels for all items identified, resulting in uneven total numbers in the sample. While this may have reflected the respondent's belief that a particular item was not important enough to warrant a score, the end result was that the ranking was not included in the analysis. Mean ratings for each of the identified items appear in Tables 1–4. Items that do not have mean scores were added after the survey by the author or by the respondents and were therefore not available for rating in the survey.

The results are limited in that the respondents were predominantly gerontological nursing educators. No effort was made to obtain demographic data as to length of time in the field or other indicators of expertise. The sample does not reflect nurses working in the field as

---

[26] J. A. Ferrario, personal communication, July 11, 1984.

[27] H. T. Brower, "The Nursing Curriculum for Long-Term Institutional Care," National League for Nursing, *op. cit.*, pp. 46–64.

Sullivan's study did.[28] Nevertheless, the findings validate earlier conjectures that nursing faculty teaching gerontological nursing demonstrate a wide disparity in their perceptions of what is or is not important. For example, one educator, who is responsible for teaching in a master's program in gerontological nursing, gave low ratings to nursing and pathological knowledge competencies, with the exception of pathopsychological issues, but rated policy and normative items high in importance. Another educator, who is responsible for teaching both master's and doctoral gerontological nursing students, did not feel that sociocultural concepts are age related, with the exception of social theories and demography, but that they are basic to all nursing. Many nurse gerontologists, as evidenced by the ratings of the rest of the respondents, would disagree. It is true, for example, that climatic conditions affect people of all ages, but they must be considered in light of the narrower thermoregulatory parameters in the aged. And certainly, retirement is a developmental life passage for older persons.

The most positive aspects of the survey were the input provided by correspondence and the additional items suggested. Not all the suggested items were added to the lists in the tables because of the author's own perceptions. Several strategic comments were made in the correspondence. According to one respondent:

> In the baccalaureate program a knowledge of the physical, psychosocial, and sociocultural aspects of aging is essential; however, the level of knowledge expected would be far different from the expectations at the master's and doctoral levels. The application of the concepts in the care of the elderly would also be quite different. Research aspects can best be specified in relation to utilization of research versus designing and implementing research on the master's and doctoral levels. In the area of political community activities, the level of baccalaureate knowledge would be that of an introduction versus the master's and doctoral level students, who should have the background to take an active part in the activities.[29]

Another respondent noted that normal aging should be taught at the undergraduate level with an emphasis on clinical application, adding:

> In addition, selected critical problem areas for which the elderly are at risk or have commonly need to be emphasized. I would see the latter as Mental Health Problems—confusion, depression, suicide; Functional Problems—falls, incontinence, immobility; and Physiological Problems—drug reactions/interactions, pressure sores. I would see the focus at the undergraduate level on adequate assessment, intervention based on what is known or logical, and appropriate referral.

[28] Sullivan, *op. cit.*

[29] P. L. Demuth, personal communication, July 19, 1984.

At the graduate level, I believe an in-depth review of normal aging based on the research literature is necessary. Common biopsychosocial problems of the aged should be analyzed from an epidemiological, basic, and applied research point of view, both in nursing and related literature. Emphasis should be on model practical derived from clinical reality tempered by research findings.

At the doctoral level, the need is to define and study a problem area in gerontological nursing through synthesis of related theory and knowlege of research methodologies. Leadership should be more comprehensively understood and practiced with foci on power and communication.[30]

Most of the respondents stressed, either through correspondence or by writing on the survey instruments, that a doctoral candidate who is studying and performing research in gerontological nursing must have a strong background in the field through master's preparation.

Burnside believes that life review and reminiscing should be differentiated, with the latter belonging at the baccalaureate level and life review at master's and doctoral levels. She further notes:

There is some content that *must* be taught from nurses aides through doctoral level in my opinion—e.g., management of Sundowner's, wandering behavior, behaviors in Alzheimer states, vigilance for drug-related problems, dehydration, prevention of falls, use of restraints, handling depressed patients, suicidal patients, . . . the most prevalent chronic illnesses, e.g. arthritis, strokes, etc., [and] relocation trauma.[31]

CLINICAL STRUCTURING

Given the diversity of nursing education, we may never reach a state of consensus on the concerns of clinical and theoretical structuring of gerontological nursing. A critical component of clinical teaching that should be included in all basic programs, however, is the use of nursing home facilities. Many basic programs fail to use this rich resource for learning opportunities. Many others continue to bring beginning students into the nursing home at a time when nursing skills and normal changes are the focus of their education. The nursing home is not the setting to teach normative aging concepts. Prevalence does not confer normality. Whether nurses consider alterations in body and health states as normal or pathological will affect their perceptions, learning, and therapeutic decision making. Some faculty insist that their students have more positive attitudes after such an experience, in spite of its seemingly inappropriate placement in the curriculum. Students' attitudes, it has been

---

[30] T. Wells, personal communication, July 12, 1984.

[31] I. M. Burnside, personal communication, June 30, 1984.

found, can be linked to the attitudes of their teachers.[32] But attitude testing alone does not test the substantive knowledge in gerontological nursing that should be expected from today's graduating nurses. Nor does it measure their choice of work upon graduation. To use an analogy, would faculty teaching pediatrics begin clinical teaching with placement in a developmental disabilities center?

Naisbitt states that "high tech" has led simultaneously to "high touch"; that is, people have responded to technological innovaitons with a resurgence of "high touch" or humanized phenomena.[33] For example, as our hospitals become more technological, the less we choose to be born in hospitals. We are constantly seeking more personally supportive and less technologically intensive environments[34] Naisbitt sees dehumanization and dissonance as major disadvantages to the increasing technologizing of health care. Could it be that, if nursing students were given an opportunity to explore values clarification concerning the aged, more would choose to work with the aged, both in nursing homes and community settings? That choice could be perceived as a humanistic backlash to the high technology nursing that is currently of interest to the majority of new graduates. If nursing faculty designed a course for students to learn about the phenomena of chronicity and chronic health problems, clinical placements could be planned in a number of settings that would promote the concept of long-term care using a continuum approach. Or, faculty could inject geriatric/gerontological nursing theory into the curriculum when students are assigned to critical care, where most patients are older.

The amount of theoretical content could most appropriately be taught in an integrated curriculum model, as evidenced in the outlined knowledge competencies. The integrated model would appropriately begin with normative aging concepts, using clinical sites such as private homes, senior citizens' centers, nutrition sites, or high-rise apartments for older people. Nursing concepts can be integrated throughout all levels of the curriculum, but a student's sophistication and increasing depth of knowledge can be augmented by learning about pathological aging in settings where people experiencing these alterations are found. The traditional medical-surgical courses, now more frequently called adult health, seem to neglect the majority of ill persons—the old. Case studies, used increasingly as simulation examples, should reflect the aged patient and the unique presentations and treatment modalities of such cases. Acute-care settings, as well as nursing home settings, are superb sites

[32] M. J. Wilhite and D. M. Johnson, "Changes in Nursing Students' Stereotypic Attitudes Toward Old People," *Nursing Research*, 25 (1976), pp. 430–432.

[33] J. Naisbitt *Megatrends: Ten New Directions Transforming Our Lives* (New York: Warner Books, 1982), p. 42.

[34] Special Committee on Aging, *op. cit.*, p. ix.

to use for the clinical teaching of pathophysiology, psychopathology, and advanced nursing care of the elderly.

In sum, the complexity of curricular issues for the integration of gerontological nursing curricula may leave the timid or novice curriculum engineer in a state of despair. At this point, however, the question is long overdue. What is to be included and how curricula is to be structured rests with the inclination and expertise of faculty. A commitment to do more is a start. No matter what the experts prescribe, what works for some will not work for others. We can only hope that these debates will no longer be necessary by the year 2000, when all nursing programs will include substantially more curricula in gerontological nursing.

Table 1. Knowledge Competency Ratings for Content on Normative Aging

Areas of Knowledge	Under-graduate	Graduate	Doctoral
I. Physical changes of aging			
A. Structural changes	4.8	4.8	3.7
1. Sensory	4.8	4.6	3.7
2. Skin	4.8	4.6	3.5
3. Muscle	4.8	4.6	3.5
4. Connective tissue	4.8	4.6	3.5
5. Organ	5.0	4.6	3.5
6. Bone resorption*			
7. Cellular*			
B. Functional changes			
1. Oxygenation and circulation	4.6	4.6	3.3
2. Thermoregulatory performance	4.6	4.6	3.3
3. Changes in absorption, excretion, metabolism, elimination	4.8	4.6	3.0
4. Fluid and electrolyte	4.8	4.6	3.3
5. Mobility	4.8	4.6	3.8
6. Response time	4.6	4.6	3.7
7. Sleep patterns	4.6	4.6	3.7
8. Neurological*			
9. Energy levels*			
II. Sexual competency	4.5	4.5	3.3
III. Immunocompetence	4.6	4.7	3.6
IV. Psychological aspects			
A. Psychological theories of aging (developmental, personality, and behavioral theories)	4.6	4.9	3.9
B. Cognition and aging	4.7	4.8	3.9
C. Attitudes toward aging and one's own aging	4.3	4.7	3.6
D. Personality development	4.2	4.8	3.9
E. Aging developmental tasks	4.2	4.8	3.9
F. Time orientation	3.8	4.9	4.0
G. Self-concept/self-esteem of older person	4.3	4.9	4.0
H. Communication styles (apraxia articulation)	4.7	4.9	4.0
I. Life satisfaction/morals*			

Areas of Knowledge	Under-graduate	Graduate	Doctoral
V. Genetics of aging	3.3	4.3	3.9
VI. Biological theories of aging	4.6	4.8	4.3
VII. Sociocultural aspects			
A. Social theories of aging (disengagement, interactionist, activities theories, etc.)	4.6	4.4	4.1
B. Family and social support system	4.3	4.6	4.0
C. Climatic conditions	4.0	4.0	3.7
D. Neighborhood	4.0	4.3	3.7
E. Role changes	4.0	4.4	4.5
F. Living arrangements	4.1	4.3	3.7
G. Life-style	4.2	4.4	4.0
H. Retirement	3.7	4.4	3.8
I. Cultural/ethnic influences	4.5	4.5	4.1
J. Demography of the aged	3.7	4.5	3.9
K. Spirituality dimensions	4.5	4.4	3.7
L. Leisure activities	4.4	4.3	3.3
VIII. Nutritional needs for older adults	4.8	4.7	4.4

* Not included in survey.

Table 2. Knowledge Competency Ratings for Content on Pathological Aging

Areas of Knowledge	Under-graduate	Graduate	Doctoral
I. Chronic health problems			
A. Interaction of multiple problems	4.5	4.8	4.0
B. Pathophysiology	4.5	4.8	3.7
C. Paliative factors	4.4	4.6	3.7
D. Medical treatment options	3.3	4.6	3.5
E.. Specific nursing management	4.4	4.8	4.0
F. Pharmacotherapy	4.4	4.8	4.0
G. Iatrogenesis	4.4	4.6	4.0
II. Active health problems			
A. Unique presentations	3.9	4.8	3.9
B. Morbidity statistics	3.9	4.8	3.9
C. Trauma	4.0	4.9	3.8
1. Burns	4.1	4.8	3.5
2. Falls	4.6	5.0	3.8
3. Risk factors	4.5	5.0	3.8
D. Acute exacerbations of chronic health problems	4.0	4.6	3.4
E. Specific nursing management	4.7	4.6	4.2
F. Pharmacotherapy	4.1	4.2	4.0
G. Iatrogenesis	4.2	4.6	3.7
III. Psychological problems			
A. Confusional states	4.8	4.9	4.2
1. Physiological bases	4.5	4.9	4.3
2. Reversible cause	4.5	4.9	4.2
3. Irreversible causes	4.5	4.9	4.0
B. Alzheimer's and other primary degenerative types	4.4	4.4	4.3
1. Pathophysiology*			
2. Differential diagnosis*			
3. DMSD classifications	4.0	4.0	4.3
D. Sleep disorders	4.4	4.9	4.1
E. Depression	4.6	5.0	4.3
F. Cognitive impairment	4.6	5.0	4.3
G. Suicide	4.5	5.0	4.1
H. Learned helplessness	3.9	4.5	4.0
I. Widowhood, grief, bereavement	4.9	4.8	4.3

Areas of Knowledge	Under-graduate	Graduate	Doctoral
J. Translocation/relocation shock	3.5	4.9	4.3
K. Effects of multiple stressors	4.4	5.0	4.0
L. Substance abuse	4.3	5.0	4.1
M. Sexual dysfunction	4.0	4.9	4.3
N. Sundowner's syndrome*			
O. Wandering behavior*			
IV. Sociocultural problems			
A. Maladaptation to dependency needs	4.1	5.0	4.1
B. Isolation, withdrawal	4.1	5.0	4.3
C. Level of and percentage of poverty victims	3.9	4.4	3.6
D. Cumulative losses	4.5	5.0	4.0
E. Inadequate support system	4.2	4.8	4.0
F. Victimization and abuse	4.2	5.0	4.0

* Not included in survey.

Table 3. Knowledge Competency Ratings for Content on Nursing

Areas of Knowledge	Under-graduate	Graduate	Doctoral
I. Gerontological Nursing Theory			
A. Gerontological nursing research	3.3	5.0	5.0
1. Review of gerontological nursing research	3.1	4.8	5.0
2. Critique of gerontological nursing research*			
3. Replication of gerontological nursing research	2.2	4.1	4.7
4. Initiating gerontological nursing research	1.8	4.2	5.0
5. Ethical issues in gerontological nursing research	2.9	4.6	5.0
B. Nursing conceptual frameworks			
1. Use in gerontological nursing research	2.4	4.7	5.0
2. Development of gerontological nursing models	2.0	4.4	5.0
C. Multidisciplinary research	2.0	3.6	5.0
D. Issues in gerontological nursing			
1. Gerontological nursing history	3.8	4.8	4.8
2. Gerontological nursing education	3.7	4.6	4.7
a. Continuing education	2.5	4.7	4.4
b. Credentialing	3.0	4.6	4.4
c. State of the art	3.7	4.5	4.7
3. Attitudes	4.6	4.8	3.8
4. Nursing manpower needs	3.5	4.7	4.4
5. Reimbursement*			
6. Gerontological nursing leadership*			
E. Gerontological nursing practice			
1. Sites, models*			
2. Standards	4.3	4.8	4.4
II. Assessment of the older client			
A. Interviewing skills	4.6	4.7	3.3
B. Comprehensive nursing history	4.7	4.7	3.3
C. Comprehensive health history	4.4	4.8	3.5
D. Comprehensive physical assessment	4.0	4.5	3.0
E. Mental status examination	4.5	4.8	3.6
F. Functional assessments	4.6	4.8	3.9
G. Development assessment*			

Areas of Knowledge	Under-graduate	Graduate	Doctoral
H. Support system assessment*			
I. Development of new assessment instruments*			
III. Institutional assessment			
A. Analysis of assessment tools for:			
1. Nursing homes	2.2	4.5	3.6
2. Sheltered care environments	2.2	4.4	3.4
3. Adult day care centers*			
B. Development of assessment tools*			
C. Utilization of assessment tools*			
IV. Assessment of home environment			
V. Nursing diagnosis of older clients*			
A. Interprets assessments*			
B. Applies research findings*			
VI. Nursing planning health care for the older client			
A. Nursing case management concepts	3.8	4.8	4.1
B. Nursing care planning conferences	3.9	4.7	4.2
C. Interdisciplinary care planning conferences	3.3	4.9	4.2
D. Nursing rounds	3.9	4.6	3.7
E. Discharge planning	3.9	4.7	3.8
F. Planning at local, state, national levels	2.8	4.7	4.4
VII. Nursing interventions for the older client			
A. Health promotion activities	4.4	5.0	3.0
1. Health teaching of older clients/significant others	4.5	4.9	3.8
2. Counseling older clients/ significant others	4.1	4.9	3.8
B. Advocacy activities	4.8	4.0	1.6
1. Individual client	4.2	4.4	4.1
2. Groups of older adults	3.3	4.1	4.3
3. Grey Panther activities	3.0	3.8	3.9

Areas of Knowledge	Under-graduate	Graduate	Doctoral
4. Retirment groups, i.e., AARP, NRTA	3.0	4.3	4.2
5. Teaching about aging			
a. Older clients and significant others	4.0	4.4	3.4
b. Nurses	2.5	4.7	3.9
c. Health professionals	1.6	4.2	4.0
d. Society	3.1	4.6	4.1
6. Residence councils	2.9	4.4	3.0
7. Self-support groups	3.0	4.2	3.4
C. Improvment of function and coping ability			
1. Rehabilitative activities			
a. Restorative activities	4.3	4.5	4.0
b. Maintenance of functional capacity	4.5	4.5	4.0
2. Exercise programs	4.5	4.4	3.7
3. Grief/bereavement work	4.0	4.6	4.1
4. Group work (reminiscence, socialization, music)	3.6	4.8	3.9
5. Life review*			
6. Environmental manipulation	4.3	4.7	3.0
a. Territoriality and personal space principles	4.1	4.9	4.1
b. Environmental orientation supports	4.2	4.8	4.0
c. Environmental socialization supports	4.2	4.8	4.0
d. Space planning	3.3	5.0	4.2
e. Safety factors	4.5	4.9	4.0
f. Use of restraints*			
7. Dying care	4.4	5.0	3.8
D. Nursing case management			
1. Strengthening and supplementing supports	4.2	4.2	4.6
2. Identifying gaps in supports	3.3	4.7	4.2
3. Tracking, coordination, and systematic reassessment	3.1	4.6	4.0
4. Information and referral	3.9	4.6	3.6
E. Assisting and supporting functioning			
1. Support measures	4.5	4.8	4.1

Areas of Knowledge	Under-graduate	Graduate	Doctoral
2. Cognitive (sensory stimulation programs (R.O., activity groups)	3.8	5.0	4.0
3. Replenishing or replacing resources or supports	3.4	4.8	3.0
4. Protective measures	3.9	4.8	3.9
5. Develops new measures*			
VIII. Nutritional evaluation			
A. Evaluation of client care	4.7	4.9	4.6
B. Evaluation of health care system for older persons	2.6	5.0	4.8
C. Quality assurance programs	2.9	5.0	4.7
D. Drug monitoring systems	3.9	5.0	4.6
E. Outcome measurements*			

* Not included in survey.

Table 4. Knowledge Competency Ratings for Content on Policy Considerations

Areas of Knowledge	Under-graduate	Graduate	Doctoral
I. Community Resources			
A. Adult day care centers	4.3	5.0	4.3
B. Home health care	4.3	5.0	4.3
C. Social supports	4.1	5.0	4.3
D. Transporation	4.1	4.9	4.2
E. Geriatric clinics	4.0	4.9	4.2·
F. Senior centers	4.2	5.0	4.2
G. Acute care geriatric evaluation units	4.0	5.0	4.3
H. Hospice care	4.0	4.9	4.3
I. Nursing homes	3.9	5.0	4.3
J. Respite care	3.9	5.0	4.3
K. Information and referral*			
L. Crisis telephone reasurrance*			
II. Legal			
A. Patient's/resident's bill of rights	4.5	4.9	3.6
B. ERISA legislation/ retirement policies	2.9	4.4	3.8
C. Guardianship/competency hearings/alternative options	3.0	4.5	3.9
D. Ethical and moral considerations	4.0	4.8	3.9
E. State and federal regulations governing residential facilities	3.6	4.4	3.7
1. Nursing homes	2.8	4.5	3.7
2. Adult congregate	2.6	4.6	3.7
F. Litigation factors	2.4	4.5	3.7
G. Wills	2.8	4.6	3.7
III. Long-term care			
A. Continuum approach	4.1	4.6	3.8
B. Options necessary	3.7	4.5	3.9
C. Case management	3.4	4.8	3.8
D. Assessment techniques	3.8	4.8	3.8
E. Issues	3.6	4.7	4.6
F. Demography of long-term care	3.9	4.8	4.1

Areas of Knowledge	Under-graduate	Graduate	Doctoral
IV. Political			
A. Public policy issues	2.6	4.5	4.7
B. Power sources	2.5	4.5	4.8
C. Hearings on aging issues	2.1	4.1	4.1
D. Bureaucratic structures	2.3	4.1	4.4
E. Partisan politics	2.2	3.8	4.2
F. Resource allocation	2.9	3.8	4.2
V. Economics			
A. Personal income	3.3	4.1	3.5
B. SSI	3.3	4.1	3.5
C. Public assistance (food stamps)	3.3		3.4
D. Social Security	3.3	4.1	3.5
E. Medicare/Medicaid	3.3	4.2	3.6
F. Supplemental health insurance	3.0	4.0	3.6
G. Grant writing*			
H. Local funding sources*			
I. Federal and foundation sources*			
VI. Housing			
A. Overview of types and adequacy	2.9	4.2	3.4
B. HUD housing	2.6	4.2	3.1
C. Life care environments	2.7	4.3	3.1
D. Sheltered care environments	3.1	4.6	3.6
E. Nursing homes	4.3	4.7	3.3
VII. Agency Support			
A. Area Agencies on Aging	3.4	4.4	4.0
B. Federal level agencies	3.1	3.9	4.0
1. HCFA	2.3	3.9	4.0
2. NIA	2.5	4.0	4.0
3. NIH	2.5	3.8	4.0
4. Division of Nursing	2.7	4.3	4.1
5. AOA	2.6	4.4	3.6

Areas of Knowledge	Under-graduate	Graduate	Doctoral
C. Local level agencies	2.9	4.0	3.9
1. State level	3.3	4.0	3.9
2. Metropolitan level	3.3	4.4	4.6
D. Health planning for the aged	3.1	4.4	4.7
E. Accessibility and availability issues	3.2	4.0	3.8
F. Ombudsman programs	3.5	4.5	4.0

* Not included in survey.

CORE CONTENT IN GEROPSYCHIATRIC NURSING

BEVERLY A. BALDWIN, RN, PhD
Assistant Professor, School of Nursing
Graduate Program
University of Maryland
Baltimore, Maryland

The health care system in this country has undergone rapid change during the last two decades. Analysis of recent trends reflects both economic and social pressures on the structure of health care services and on the providers of these services. Many simultaneous changes have created strain on traditional roles and values and have altered the nature and dimensions of social needs. Nowhere are the changes more evident or far-reaching than in long-term care of the elderly.

Demographic projections indicate that by the year 2000, the U.S. population will total 260.4 million, with 32 million people age 65 years or older; the number of those over the age of 85 will reach 3.8 million.[1] Although only 5 percent of the 25.6 million Americans now over the age of 65 are confined to institutions for physical or emotional care, at least one in five older adults may be found in a long-term care facility on any one day. Those over the age of 85 are particularly vulnerable to the complex chronic disabilities requiring institutional care. It is an-

---

[1] Institute of Medicine, Division of Mental Health and Behavioral Medicine, *Health, Behavior and Aging* (Washington, D.C.: National Academy Press, 1981); Health Care Financing Administration, *Long-Term Care: Background and Future Directions* (Washington, D.C.: U.S. Department of Health and Human Services, 1981); and Robert N. Butler and Myrna I. Lewis, *Aging and Mental Health* (3rd ed.; St. Louis, MO: C. V. Mosby Co., 1982.

ticipated that by 2030, 2.6 million older adults will be in nursing homes, more than double the number in nursing homes today.[2]

The present and projected needs for long-term care services for adults over the age of 65 far exceed the number of health care professionals providing those services. Currently, only 5 percent of all nursing home personnel are registered nurses. Of the one million employed registered nurses, less than 9 percent work in nursing homes or other long-term care facilities for the elderly. Although physician coverage for nursing homes is required by law, estimates suggest that primary care physicians who treat adults spend less than 2 percent of their time in direct patient contact with their patients in nursing homes.[3] The inadequate number of health care professionals involved in long-term care for the elderly demonstrates the widening gap between the requirements for a specific type of service within the health care system and the personnel available to deliver the care.

Investigators cite numerous possible reasons for lack of interest by professional nurses in long-term care of older adults. Three of the areas frequently addressed are inadequate financial incentives, the nature of the work setting, and the role ambiguity of the professional nurse in long-term care.

Most long-term care settings (including home health care agencies) pay lower salaries and offer fewer benefits for nurses than do hospitals. In recent surveys of registered nurses employed full time, staff nurses in nursing homes were found to make an average annual salary of $14,332, representing 82 percent of the mean salary of $17,393 for all full-time registered nurses and 87 percent of the mean salary of $16,451 for all staff nurses employed full time in acute-care hospital settings.[4]

The organization and structure of long-term care facilities for the elderly, particularly nursing homes, pose unique problems for the professional nurse. Characteristics of the work setting include only 1.5 licensed health care providers for every 100 patients; an estimated annual turnover rate of 80 to 100 percent among the untrained and unlicensed employees who deliver over 90 percent of the care; and a structural design patterned after acute-care hospitals, in which the patient is expected to remain in bed and become socially isolated from staff and other patients.[5]

---

[2] Butler and Lewis, *op. cit.*

[3] Linda H. Aiken, "Nursing Priorities for the 1980's: Hospitals and Nursing Homes," *American Journal of Nursing,* 81, No. 2 (1981), pp. 324–330; and B. Valdeck, "Nursing Homes: A National Problem," in Aiken, ed., *Nursing in the 1980's: Crises, Opportunities and Challenges* (Philadelphia: J. B. Lippincott, 1982).

[4] Aiken, *op. cit.;* Health Care Financing Administration, *op. cit.;* and W. Scanlon and J. Feder, "The Long-Term Care Marketplace: An Overview," *Healthcare Financial Management,* 14, No. 1 (1984), pp. 18–36.

[5] Aiken, *op. cit.;* Butler and Lewis, *op. cit.;* and E. M. Shields and E. Kick, "Nursing Care in Nursing Homes," in Aiken, ed., *op. cit.,* pp. 195–210.

The possibility for nurses to assess and intervene in psychosocial and geropsychiatric problems of patients in these settings is limited.

Role ambiguity surrounding nursing practice in long-term care has been attributed to a number of factors. Shields and Kick suggest that the reimbursement mechanisms for long-term care influence the role expression of the nurse.[6] Reimbursement for nursing home care (Medicare and Medicaid) does not recognize the contribution of professional nursing because the medical model orientation dominates the system. The role nurses assume in those settings is dictated by the financial system supporting long-term care.

Aiken, on the other hand, contends that role ambiguity of nurses in long-term care stems from the fact that most of the facilities are physically and professionally isolated from academic health settings and teaching hospitals.[7] A national demonstration project, funded by the Robert Wood Johnson Foundation, is now underway to implement and evaluate affiliation between schools of nursing and long-term care facilities.

Other explanations suggest that the inadequate number of nurses with advanced preparation in gerontological nursing contribute to the lack of role articulation in long-term care.[8] The mandate for nursing to increase the number and level of clinicians prepared for long-term care is clear in this as well as other analyses of nursing's role in gerontology.[9]

Although role ambiguity of nurses in long-term care may account, along with the other explanations, for the inadequate number of nurses who choose gerontological nursing as a specialty area for practice, even fewer nurses express interest in or knowledge of the geropsychiatric problems of the elderly requiring long-term care.[10]

Mental illness is more prevalent in the elderly than in younger adults. It has been estimated that 15 to 25 percent of older adults have significant mental health problems.[11] The incidence of psychosis increases after age 65 and even more beyond age 75. Twenty-five percent of all reported suicides in the United States are committed by persons over the age of 65.[12] Depression is a significant problem for the elderly. Prevalence rates

---

[6] Shields and Kick, *op. cit.*

[7] Aiken, *op. cit.*

[8] Institute of Medicine, Division of Health Care Services, *Nursing and Nursing Education* (Washington, D.C.: National Academy Press, 1983).

[9] I. M. Martinson, "Gerontological Nursing." Statement presented to the National Advisory Council on Aging (Bethesda, MD: National Institute on Aging, 1980).

[10] *Ibid.;* and American Nurses' Association, *Facts About Nursing: '82–83* (Kansas City, MO: ANA).

[11] Federal Council on the Aging, *Mental Health and the Elderly: Recommendations for Action*, Reports of the President's Commission on Mental Health Task Panel on the Elderly and the Secretary's Committee on the Mental Health and Illness of the Elderly, Pub. No. (OHDS) 80–20960 (Washington, D.C.: U.S. Government Printing Office, 1979).

[12] *Ibid.;* and L. D. Breslan and M. R. Haug, *Depression and Aging* (New York: Springer Publishing Co., 1983).

of psychiatric diagnoses of depressive disorders alone range from 8 to 10 percent for the elderly living in the community. However, prevalence of the transient but often dysfunctional symptoms of depression is estimated as high as 45 percent by some researchers and clinicians.[13] Severe forms of senile dementia, including Alzheimer's disease, affects more than one million older persons and reduces longevity almost two-thirds after onset. Another two million elderly may have mild to moderate forms of these diseases.[14]

The interaction of chronic disability, which affects about 85 percent of older adults, and financial difficulties, which affect one out of seven older adults, contributes to increasing stress. Although the stresses that affect the mental health of the elderly are not necessarily unique, they are many and pervasive, and are often devastating to both the elderly and their families.

THE AT-RISK ELDERLY

Multiple personal losses often accompany advancing age, including the loss of spouse, family, friends, and even children. Fourteen percent of men between 65 and 75 years of age are widowed; in the group over age 75, the rate increases to 25 percent.[15] Fifty-four percent of all women over age 65 are widows, and of the women over 75 years, 70 percent have lost their spouses.

Social and interpersonal isolation may also contribute to increased stress and mental health problems. Approximately one out every seven men and one out of every three women over 65 live alone. Over one million older adults—5 percent of this population—are confined to institutions for long-term care. Among those age 75 or older, 10 percent are institutionalized, and 20 percent of those 85 and older are confined to a long-term care setting.

The older adult residing in an institutional setting—whether an acute-care hospital or a nursing home or extended care facility—faces stresses that place him or her at risk for mental health problems. Eighty-six percent of older adults have chronic health problems, which are multiple in nature, with at least three million being serious. Loss of or diminished physical health, whether due to cardiovascular, respiratory, or

---

[13] Butler and Lewis, *op. cit.*; R. Levy and F. Post, eds., *The Psychiatry of Late Life* (Boston; Blackwell Scientific Publications, 1982); "The Elderly Remain in Need of Mental Health Services," Report No. GAO/HRD-82-112 (Washington, D.C.: U.S. General Accounting Office, 1982).

[14] E. Busse and D. G. Blazer, eds., Handbook of Geriatric Psychiatry (New York: Van Nostrand, 1980); W. E. Kelly, ed., *Alzheimer's Disease and Related Disorders* (Springfield, IL: Charles C. Thomas, Publisher, 1984); and B. A. Wilson and N. Moffat, *Clinical Management of Memory Problems* (Rockville, MD: Aspen Publications, 1984).

[15] Federal Council on the Aging, *op. cit.*; and "The Elderly Should Benefit from Expanded Home Health Care but Increasing These Services Will Not Insure Cost Reductions," Report No. HGAD/IPE-83-1 (Washington, D.C.: U.S. General Accounting Office, 1982).

musculoskeletal diseases, increases stress and can produce significant psychological reactions for many older adults. Decreased mobility, which affects approximately 20 percent of all people over age 65, contributes to isolation and increased stress from both psychobiological and psychosocial perspectives.

Older adults requiring acute care may encounter multiple stressors, which often result in mental or cognitive problems, including confusion, disorientation, alterations in memory, and depression. The longer the hospitalization, the greater the likelihood of mental health problems occurring and becoming chronic.[16]

The prevalence of symptoms of mental illness among nursing home residents is high, with estimates ranging from 50 to 75 percent.[17] Although the elderly have the lowest rate of new admissions to state and county mental hospitals, they constitute 25 percent of the patients residing in those facilities. The institutionalized elderly are at risk for developing chronic mental health problems since aggressive psychiatric treatment modalities are infrequently used for this age group in these settings.

Elderly people and their families residing in the community also represent at-risk groups for mental health problems. Since 1965, the community mental health movement has reinforced the concept of deinstitutionalization of patients in state and county mental hospitals. For 40 percent of the elderly people who are discharged from mental hospitals, the next step is referral to a nursing home.[18] Many others are released into the community, to become single room occupants in hotels or boarding houses. Follow-up care for this group is inadequate, and data are limited regarding their long-term status.

Although the majority of older adults in this country are financially comfortable, poverty puts many older adults at risk for mental health problems. Income can drop by 50 to 75 percent with retirement. Estimates suggest that one out every seven older persons lives below the U.S. Census Bureau's poverty level, including one out of every three older women living alone.[19] The older impoverished woman, usually black, is at high risk for both physical and mental health problems and underutilizes community health services. Financial limitations affect nutritional status, medical compliance (especially with medications and prescribed treatments), and resources for coping with the stress of illness (e.g., adequate housing and transporation).

Families of elderly people may also experience emotional problems

---

[16] M. O. Wolanin and L. R. F. Phillips, *Confusion: Prevention and Care* (St. Louis, MO: C. V. Mosby Co., 1981).

[17] Butler and Lewis, *op. cit.;* and Valdeck, *op. cit.*

[18] Federal Council on the Aging, *op. cit.*

[19] "The Elderly Should Benefit from Expanded Home Health Care."

as part of their caregiving role.[20] Forty percent of all primary caregivers in the family are women and live in the same household with the older person or in close proximity.[21] The many demands of work, home, and family responsibilities on this group are compounded by required changes in life-style, lack of privacy, and feelings of resentment, guilt, and, for some, being "trapped."

In a research project currently being conducted by this author at the University of Maryland in collaboration with Dr. Karen Kleeman, stress-management groups are being examined using family caregivers of elderly individuals enrolled in adult day care centers. These caregivers experience a great deal of stress related to the caregiver role, as demonstrated by a high level of psychosomatic problems (e.g., insomnia, headaches, and gastrointestinal problems), days lost from work, and feelings of depression and despair. The limitations in the professional resources available to these families add to the stress and frustration of keeping the frail older person in the home. The caregivers found incontinence and confusion of the older person particularly stressful. Not only are these behaviors disruptive to the family, but the cargivers' lack of knowledge about effectively intervening in these problems adds to their frustration.

A national study of community mental health centers conducted to determine their utilization by the elderly found that less than 4 percent of the clients seen in these centers are over the age of 65.[22] Less than 2 percent of clients seen in private clinics for elderly. Outreach, case finding, and special services for this age group are not generally available. The underutilization of mental health services by this age group is due to the attitudes of both the elderly and the health professionals. Older adults resist mental health explanations as rationales for their problems and may refuse treatment. Conversely, many health professionals, particularly in mental health, think the elderly are not amenable to treatment; therefore, they do not seek out elderly people who could benefit from a wide range of mental health services.

CLINICAL PRACTICE

Advancing age is associated with the onset of long-term chronic illnesses that are largely incurable given present knowledge. Vladeck suggests that since many of the chronic ailments of the elderly are intractable to modern medical science, the practitioner should focus on preventive

---

[20] P. V. Rabins et al., "The Impact of Dementia on the Family," *Journal of the American Medical Association,* 248 (1982), pp. 333–335.

[21] New York State Office for the Aging, *Family Caregiving and the Elderly: Policy Recommendations and Research Findings* (Albany, NY: New York State Office for the Aging, 1983).

[22] "The Elderly Remain in Need of Mental Health Services."

and maintenance strategies that maximize the potential of the older person for psychosocial as well as physical functioning.[23]

As one grows older, the fundamental interaction of physical, medical, psychosocial, and emotional problems becomes more evident and, for many, more complex in nature.[24] There is greater interdependence of dysfunction; consequently, when the elderly become physically ill they are more likely to experience related social and emotional problems. Conversely, as an aging individual experiences increasing psychosocial losses, the onset of physical illnesses may be accelerated and accentuated. The care of the sick aged becomes a problem within the social care system rather than the highly technical health care system. Nursing is in a unique position to bridge the gap between these two systems and to offer the older adult an opportunity to function at his or her maximum potential.

Historically, the approach used by nursing for identifying and meeting patients' needs reflects a reliance on the physician's definition of patients' problems and modes of intervention. The medical model focuses on diseases and the specialized procedures for dealing with them. It persists primarily because it is backed by a vast and well-accepted medical science and technology. Most physicians, regardless of area of specialization, concentrate on needs of the patient that are pathologically derived and rely on knowledge and skills developed in the biophysical sciences to meet those needs.

Although nurses frequently assume some responsibility for determining the diagnosis and treatment of pathological conditions in patients, the major responsibility and ultimate legal authority in this area remains within the jurisdiction of medical practice. Nurses receive training in the biophysical aspects of patient care and often form opinions regarding the nature of a patient's physical pathology and the appropriate type of treatment. However, because of the professional hierarchy found in the settings in which most nurses practice and the long-standing subordinate relationship of nurses to physicians, the impact nurses have on altering the medical model may be limited. The exception may be long-term care, in which the conspicious absence of physicians facilitates the nurse's integration of the biophysical and psychosocial components of care. However, as Shields and Kick suggest, the components of care that are unique to nursing—that of health assessment and promotion, disease prevention, development of nursing care plans, and patient education—are not among the services that qualify for reimbursement.[25] The extent to which nurses can focus on mental health needs of the elderly in the long-term setting is to some extent, therefore, determined by the system itself.

---

[23] Valdeck, *op. cit.*

[24] Butler and Lewis, *op. cit.*

[25] Shields and Kick, *op. cit.*

In the early 1950s, with the assistance of social and behavioral scientists, nurses initiated concentrated efforts toward defining the psychosocial perspective for nursing practice. These efforts are significant for nurses dealing with mental health needs of older adults, because the focus of these innovative clinicians and researchers was on the way in which a patient perceived his or her situation, including but not limited to the medical condition, the prognosis, and the consequences for the patient and for others of these events in the patient's life.[26] The focus on psychosocial needs of patients does not negate the fact that nurses rely on biophysical alternatives to assess and intervene in some patient problems, illustrated by the administration of medication for the promotion of sleep or the relief of pain.

Several research endeavors over the last two decades demonstrate the significance of psychosocial interventions in the mental health problems of institutional patients. The Loeb Center for Nursing and Rehabilitation, Bronx, New York, provides such an example. The traditional nursing service hierarchy has been eliminated, and all staff nurses have equal responsibility and authority. The nurse becomes the chief therapeutic agent, with other professionals, including physicians, serving as resource persons and consultants. Nursing staff are supplemented by ward clerks and messenger-attendants. Interpersonally, nurses use a nondirective approach with patients. By listening to patients and responding to requests, the nurse assists patients to assume greater responsibility for deciding matters for themselves, including activities of daily living.[27]

In 1968, a team of nurses, behavioral scientists, and a psychiatrist conducted an experimental study to measure the impact of skilled nursing care on the behavior of older physically ill patients.[28] It was hypothesized that skilled nursing care, operationalized as interaction, provides a stimulus for the patient to become active, involved, and oriented to reality and that purposeful interactions inhibit psychosocial atrophy, especially in communication, and physical decay. The findings indicated that patients receiving skilled nursing care (interaction), even in deprived institutional settings, became more involved in interactions with others and developed a more positive emotional attitude.

In a series of field experiments in nursing homes, Langer and Rodin demonstrated the impact of the institutional environment and verbal

[26] I. M. Burnside, *Working with the Elderly: Group Process and Techniques* (Duxbury, MA: Duxbury Press, 1978); D. Mechanic, "Nursing and Mental Health Care: Expanding Future Possibilities for Nursing Services," in Aiken, ed., *op. cit.,* pp. 343–358; and Beverly A. Baldwin, "Psychosocially Oriented Behavior of Gerontological Nurses in a Long-Term Care Facility," unpublished doctoral dissertation, University of Kentucy.

[27] Genrose J. Alfano, "Healing or Caretaking—Which Will It Be?" *Nursing Clinics of North America,* 6, No. 2 (1971), pp. 273–280; and Alfano, "Hospital-Based Extended Care Nursing: A Case Study of the Loeb Center," in Aiken, ed., *op. cit.,* pp. 211–228.

[28] J. M.A. Weiss, ed., *Nurses, Patients and Social Systems: The Effect of Skilled Nursing Intervention upon Institutionalized Older Patients* (Columbia: University of Missouri Press, 1968).

interactions on the elderly.[29] An intervention designed to increase feelings of choice and personal responsibility over daily events on the part of the institutionalized elderly resulted in greater mental alertness, increased involvement in activities, and a decrease in mortality rate in the experimental group. Reevaluations 18 months after the completion of the interventions indicated the environmental changes had sustained beneficial effects for the nursing home residents in the treatment group. A second study with nursing home residents revealed an improvement in residents' memory when the cognitive demands of the environment were increased and positive reinforcement was given for attending to and remembering persons, events, and environmental factors.[30]

Other interventions that have potential for meeting the mental health needs of the elderly, whether in an institution, a community agency, or the home setting, have been demonstrated and documented in either clinical practice observations or in clinical studies. Examples of some of these effective modalities include group process and group psychotherapy; reminiscence and life review; remotivation, reality orientation, and cognitive structuring; occupational, recreational, and music therapy; individual psychotherapy and counseling; exercise and movement therapies; and behavior modification.[31]

Clinical practice in geriatric mental health offers nursing unlimited opportunities to develop and test creative and innovative interventions. One well-documented observation, although not well recognized by nursing, is that the elderly respond positively to many of the traditional and well-established clinical interventions in psychiatric nursing.[32] Working with the high-risk or already mentally impaired older adult could provide an avenue for refining some of those interventions. Nursing's challenge is to develop well-designed and systematic studies to determine the nursing interventions most appropriate in meeting the specific mental health needs of the elderly.

FACULTY NEEDS

The inadequate number of nursing faculty prepared in gerontological nursing is well recognized both within and outside of the profession.

---

[29] Ellen J. Langer and Judith Rodin, "The Effects of Choice and Enhanced Personal Responsibility for the Aged: A Field Experiment in an Institutional Setting, *Journal of Personality and Social Psychology*, 34, No. 2 (1976), pp. 191–198; and Langer and Rodin, "Long-Term Effects of a Control-Relevant Intervention with the Institutionalized Aged," *Journal of Personality and Social Psychology*, 35, No. 12 (1977), pp. 897–902.

[30] Ellen J. Langer and Judith Rodin, "Environmental Determinants of Memory Improvement in Late Adulthood," *Journal of Personality and Social Psychology*, 37, No. 11 (1979), pp. 2003–2013.

[31] Burnside, *op. cit.;* Butler and Lewis, *op. cit.;* Wolanin and Phillips, *op. cit.;* Levy and Post, *op. cit.;* J. Birren and R. B. Slone, eds., *Handbook of Geriatric Psychiatry* (New York: Van Nostrand, 1980); Institute of Medicine, Division of Mental Health and Behavioral Medicine, *op. cit.;* M. Bergener, ed., *Geropsychiatric Diagnosis and Treatment* (New York: Springer Publishing Co., 1983); Bresland and Haug, *op. cit.;* and Busse and Blazer, *op. cit.*

[32] Butler and Lewis, *op. cit.*

The rapid growth of graduate programs in gerontological nursing indicates, in part, the profession's response to the need for faculty, administrators, clinical specialists, and researchers prepared in this specialty. However, the reality behind this growth in interest may be in the increased funding available for the establishment of such programs.

The shortage of adequately prepared specialists is even more severe in geropsychiatric nursing, although funding has been available for graduate programs through the National Institute of Mental Health for the last three years. Nursing's response to the request for proposals for fiscal year 1984 on clinical training programs in geriatric mental health was weak.[33] Out of the 56 proposals submitted for the March 1984 review cycle, only 6 were submitted by nursing faculty (3 for the Faculty Development Award and 3 for the Clinical Emphasis in Geriatric Mental Health Program).

Although inadequate in number to meet the present mental health needs of the elderly, several graduate programs have been developed that offer a specialty in geropsychiatric nursing or an opportunity for an emphasis or concentration in this area. Such programs are found, for example, at Frances Payne Bolton School of Nursing, Rutgers—The State University of New Jersey, University of Arkansas, University of Pennsylvania, and University of Maryland. These programs vary in scope, substantive emphasis, and curriculum length, but they provide a variety of models for integrating the specialties of psychiatric and gerontological nursing. Doctoral programs offering a specialty in geropsychiatric nursing are difficult to determine, since many schools require students to enter the doctoral program with a substantive clinical specialty obtained through a master's degree, and the recent emergence of programs in geropsychiatric nursing would limit the number of students going into a doctoral program with geriatric mental health as a defined interest.

Support for further development of graduate programs in gerontological nursing has been recently emphasized in the Institute of Medicine's report, *Nursing and Nursing Education: Public Policies and Private Actions*.[34] The degree to which nursing educators will respond to this and other governmental support of graduate programs in gerontological and geropsychiatric nursing programs remains to be seen. Many nurses still seem reluctant to recognize the need to include these specialties in the mainstream of nursing education, practice, and research.

The teaching of geropsychiatric nursing concepts at the undergraduate level in nursing remains rare, since the limited number of prepared faculty in this area precludes introduction of concepts, except in a limited

---

[33] "Announcement: Mental Health Clinical Training Grants in: Child Mental Health, Geriatric Mental Health, and Support for Minority and Disadvantaged Students" (Rockville, MD: National Institute of Mental Health, November 1983).

[34] Institute of Medicine, Division of Health Care Services, *op. cit.*

or superficial manner. Recent reports and studies suggest that a specific focus on the needs and care of the elderly is not included in most accredited undergraduate programs in nursing.[35]

Nowhere is the immediate need for programs in gerontological and geropsychiatric nursing more pressing than in continuing eduation. In a 1976 study of nursing homes, 76 percent of the directors of nursing in skilled and intermediate care nursing homes who were interviewed had a diploma in nursing as their highest academic achievement. Of those nurses, 65 percent stated that they had participated in less than nine hours of formalized continuing education on any topic in the last three years.[36] Another study of 50 nurses employed in a large Veterans Administration long-term care facility for geriatric patients noted that 80 percent of the nurses attended some formalized continuing education offering outside the facility at least once each year.[37] However, few of these programs were in geriatric/gerontological nursing, and no one had attended a program specific to the mental health needs of the geriatric patient. Martinson considers the lack of ongoing continuing education and staff development as one of the most pressing problems for clinicians in gerontological nursing.[38]

The number and variety of general continuing education programs in the fields of geriatrics and gerontology are growing. Most are projected as interdisciplinary in scope, but few address problems specific to nursing assessment and care of the elderly. Also, the offerings are usually one to two days in length and utilize the lecture format, with no follow-up or opportunity to determine how the information can be implemented in the clinical setting. Participants in these programs are seen as passive learners and have little chance to interact with the faculty or evaluate the relevance of the content to the work setting. This is particularly crucial in the areas of assessment and implementation of appropriate treatment modalities in geropsychiatric nursing. It is one thing to read or hear about the assessment of mental health needs but quite another to actually utilize standardized assessment instruments in evaluating patients in the clinical setting. Indeed, in nursing, the emphasis on physical assessment and articulation of the nurse practitioner role in primary care and other settings usually does not include mental or

---

[35] *Ibid.;* Martinson, *op. cit.;* D. W. Light, "Medical and Nursing Education: Surface Behavior and Deep Structure," in D. Mechanic, ed., *Handbook of Health, Health Care, and the Health Professions* (New York: Free Press, 1983).

[36] Center for Studies of the Mental Health of the Aging, "Care of the Mentally Ill in the Nursing Home," addendum to *National Plan for the Chronically Mentally Ill* (Rockville, MD: National Institute of Mental Health, September 1983).

[37] Baldwin, *op. cit.*

[38] Martinson, *op. cit.*

emotional assessment as part of the total assessment protocol.[39]

One exception to this more traditional type of continuing education program is the Gerontology Nurse Educator Training Program offered at the University of Maryland School of Nursing since 1979. Now in its fifth year of funding, this program offers a special type of continuing education for nurses in nursing homes, other long-term care settings, and acute-care hospitals and for faculty from schools of nursing. Participants enroll for a one-year program, in which they meet for four 2½-day workshops spaced out over the twelve-month period. National leaders in gerontological nursing provide keynote addresses on the first day of each workshop. Experts from disciplines including medicine, occupational and recreational therapy, social work, psychology, and health policy augment the nursing focus of these workshops. During the year of the program, participants are required to develop an educational program for their facility. Program staff assist in the development and implementation of these educational programs throughout the year, including site visits to the participants' facilities. In the program's fourth and fifth years, clinical practice of the participants has been emphasized. Staff have assisted in the identification of areas for practice and supervision of participants in the participants' own facilities. Approximately 200 nurses have participated in the University of Maryland program. Based on the type of facility the participants come from, it is estimated that approximately 5,000 patients have been affected by this program, either directly, through staff development or nursing care provided by the participants, or through the students taught by participants from schools of nursing.

CURRICULUM CONSIDERATIONS

Gunter and Estes have provided nurse educators with a detailed outline of content and format for varying academic levels in gerontic nursing.[40] The Gerontological Nursing Practice Division of the American Nurses' Association, through documents on standards of practice and statements on scope and the role of the gerontological nurse, provide further explanation of the scope of didactic content and clinical experiences inherent in gerontological nursing.[41] Several concerns emerge from these and other documents regarding the development of curriculum in gerontological

---

[39] *Ibid.;* Light, *op. cit.;* and Human Resources Administration, *Health Personnel Issues in the Context of Long-Term Care in Nursing Homes* (Washington, D.C.: Department of Health and Human Services, 1980).

[40] L. M. Gunter and C. A. Estes, *Education for Gerontic Nursing* (New York: Springer Pubishing Co.. 1979).

[41] American Nurses' Association, *Standards for Gerontological Nursing Practice; A Statement on the Scope of Gerontological Nursing Practice;* and *A Challenge for Change: The Role of Gerontological Nursing* (Kansas City, MO: ANA, 1976, 1981, and 1982, respectively).

and geropsychiatric nursing. Of particular interest is content specific to geropsychiatric nursing.

At the undergraduate generalist level, the focus should be not on the pathological conditions affecting the older adult but on normal aging parameters and how the deviations from normal development can be assessed, anticipated, and prevented. Traditionally, undergraduate course in growth and development do not include a focus on middle-aged and older adults. In addition, many courses in women's health and gynecology do not address the needs and problems of the menopausal and postmenopausal woman. In the author's experience as a nursing faculty member, few schools offer mental health experiences for undergraduate students in a geriatric setting (home care, day care, or long-term care institutions), nor do they offer experiences for students with older adults who are functioning independently and are in optimal health. On the contrary, the introduction of undergraduate nursing students to the care of older adults has come through experiences in nursing homes as part of fundamental skills courses.[42] These experiences proved negative for many students, since the image presented of the older adult was of a frail, often immobilized, confused, and incontinent institutionalized patient. It is encouraging to see a decrease in this type of experience.

Moreover, undergraduate faculty are recognizing that the needs of older adults requiring long-term care are complex and interactive. Special knowledge and skill in assessing and intervening in subtle problems, such as confusion, mood changes, and withdrawal, are necessary in order to provide therapeutic care. Faculty cannot teach what they do not know. The reluctance to recognize and include content on geriatric mental health in acute-care hospital settings persists, even though it has been well documented that on any one day, 40 to 80 percent of all patients admitted to an acute-care hospital are over the age of 65.[43] Confusional states are common in elderly patients with hip fracture who are admitted to acute-care hospitals, and the incidence of incontinence and depression increases with their prolonged immobilization.[44]

The rapid growth of the geropsychiatric field and the large volume of clinical research now underway in geriatric mental health provide a body of substantive knowledge for inclusion in graduate programs in nursing. Although there is currently a dearth of research in geropsychiatric nursing, the specialty is expanding from both an educational and research perspective. Clinical studies, from within and outside nursing, should be included as primary content in both master's and doc-

---

[42] Martinson, *op. cit.*

[43] Federal Council on the Aging, *op. cit.;* Aiken, *op. cit.;* and "The Elderly Should Benefit from Expanded Home Health Care."

[44] Aiken, *op. cit.;* and Wolanin and Phillips, *op. cit.*

toral programs in geropsychiatric nursing. Although nursing is less concerned with the medical diagnosis than with the clinical phenomena presented, the reality is that current priorities for governmental research funding are on specific diseases of aging and the aged.[45] Research initiatives within the National Institute of Mental Health include a recent focus on mental illness in nursing homes.[46] This research initiative resulted from a national conference on Care of the Mentally Ill in Nursing Homes, in which both nurse educators, clinicians, and researchers had significant input.[47]

The specific content to be included in graduate programs in geropsychiatric nursing depends on several factors, including the role the program is preparing the graduate to assume, the admission criteria and expectations, and the expertise of the faculty. Regardless of the type of scope of the program, graduate nursing should take advantage of the multidisciplinary nature of the specialty and the potential for interaction with other professionals providing care and conducting research on problems of mutual concern.

---

[45] Center for Studies of the Mental Health of the Aging, "Research Update on Alzheimer's Disease—1984" (Rockville, MD: National Institute of Mental Health, 1984); and Secretary's Task Force on Alzheimer's Disease, U.S. Department of Health and Human Services, *Alzheimer's Disease* (Washington, D.C.: U.S. Government Printing Office, September 1984).

[46] "Grant Announcement: Research on Mental Illness in Nursing Homes" (Rockville, MD: National Institute of Mental Health, September 1984).

[47] Center for Studies of the Mental Health of the Aging, "Care of the Mentally Ill in the Nursing Home."

BIBLIOGRAPHY

Aiken, Linda H. "Nurses." In David Mechanic, ed., *Handbook of Health, Health Care and the Health Professions*. New York: Free Press, 1983, pp. 407–413.

_____. "Nursing's Future: Public Policies, Private Actions," *American Journal of Nursing*, 83, No. 10 (1983), pp. 1440–1444.

American Academy of Nursing. *Long-Term Care in Perspective: Present and Future Directions for Nursing*. Kansas City, MO: American Nurses' Association, 1976.

American Nurses' Assocation. *Nursing: A Social Policy Statement*. Kansas City, MO: ANA, 1980.

_____. *Statement on Psychiatric and Mental Health Nursing Practice*. Kansas City, MO: ANA, 1976.

Center for Studies of the Mental Health of the Aging, *Resource Guide for Mental Health and Support Services for the Elderly*. Rockville, MD: National Institute of Mental Health, 1981.

Cohen, Gene D. "The Mental Health Professional and the Alzheimer's Patient," *Hospital and Community Psychiatry*, 35, No. 2 (February 1984), pp. 115–116, 122.

Craik, F. I. M., and S. Trehub. *Aging and Cognitive Processes*. New York: Plenum Press, 1982.

Hall, B. (Ed.). *Mental Health and the Aging*. New York: Grune and Stratton, 1984.

Kim, H., et al. *Toward the Mental Health of the Rural Elderly*. Washington, D.C.: University Press of America, 1981.

Rankin, N. M., and V. Burggraf. "Aging in the 80's," *Journal of Gerontological Nursing*, 9 (1983), p. 5.

Reif, L., and C. L. Estes. "Long-Term Care: New Opportunities for Professional Nursing." In Linda H. Aiken, ed., *Nursing in the 1980's: Crises, Opportunities and Challenges*. Philadelphia: J.B. Lippincott Co., 1982, pp. 147–182.

Reisberg, B. *Alzheimer's Disease*. New York: Free Press, 1983.

Santos, J. F., and G. R. VandenBos. *Psychology and the Older Adult: Challenges for Training in the 1980's*. Washington, D.C.: American Psychological Association, 1981.

Somers, A. "Long-Term Care for the Elderly and Disabled: A New Health Priority," *New England Journal of Medicine*, 307, No. 4 (1982), pp. 221–226.

Smits, H., et al. "Medicare's Nursing Home Benefit—Variations in Interpretation," *New England Journal of Medicine,* 307 (1982), pp. 855–862.

Steury, S., and M. L. Blank. *Readings in Psychotherapy with Older People.* Rockville, MD: Center for the Studies of Mental Health of the Aging, National Institute of Mental Health, 1980).

United States General Accounting Office. "Cost Increases and the Need for Services are Creating Problems for the States and the Elderly," Report No. GAO/IPE-84-1. Washington, D.C.: U.S. GAO, 1983.

Valdeck, B. "Understanding Long-Term Care," *New England Journal of Medicine,* 307, No. 14 (1982), pp. 889–890.

————. *Unloving Care,* New York: Basic Books, 1980.

White House Conference on Aging. *Final Report: White House Conference on Aging—1981.* Bethesda, MD: White House Conference on Aging, 1981.

Zarit, S. H. *Aging and Mental Disorders.* New York: Free Press, 1980.

CARING: A CONCEPT WITHIN NURSING

LAVERNE GALLMAN, RN, PhD
Chairperson, Graduate Program
School of Nursing
University of Texas at Austin
Austin, Texas

Historically, when we look at nursing we see an activity in which the participants provide assistance to those in need. Some people believe that it is a "calling." Others believe that it is a profession with a foundation based on scientific research, which provides meaning and guidance in assisting individuals to achieve optimum wellness. To achieve the goal of assisting a person in reaching a high level of wellness requires what is perhaps the core of nursing: caring.

A search of the literature to attempt to determine the meaning of this concept in nursing revealed that caring was not itself identified as a subject. It was submused under nursing or nursing care. The concept of caring seems to be taken for granted in nursing; however, its meaning remains elusive. If we had a clearer understanding of caring, we would have a better foundation for identifying what might be categorized as caring behaviors.

"Care confronts us with the deeper meanings of our lives."[1] With the advent of high technology in our society, some writers are emphasizing the need for more humane approaches. Naisbitt calls this the "high

---

[1] Myron Ebersole, "Courage to Care," *Mennonite Medical Messenger*, 33, No. 4 (December 1982), pp. 19-22.

tech/high touch'' formula. He believes that ''whenever new technology is introduced into society, there must be a counterbalancing human response.''[2] There is thus a growing need to analyze the concept of caring and to test this part of the theoretical framework of nursing. As more people become interested in the concept, the 1980s offer the opportunity to focus on research related to caring. In our society, this implies research in an intercultural, multiethnic environment that has change as a constant.

This analysis will attempt to clarify the meaning of the concept of caring. With more clarification, perhaps an operational definition can be developed. Moreover, as more individuals attempt to clarify the concept, the results may lead to research that adds to existing theory in nursing.

DEFINITIONS

As an intransitive verb, *Webster's New World Dictionary* defines *care* as:

(1) to have objection, worry, regret, mind [Do you mind if I go?] (2) to feel concern or interest [to care about others] (3) to feel love or a liking [for] (4) to take charge of; to look after; provide for (5) to wish [for]; want.

As a transitive verb, care has the following definition:

(1) to feel concern about or interest in, (2) to wish or desire.
—*have a care:* to be careful or cautious
—*take care; take care of:* (1) to have charge of or be responsible for; look after; attend to; (2) to provide for; protect against trouble, want.

Synonyms:
    Care—suggests a weighing down of the mind, as by dread, apprehension, or great responsibility.
    Concern—suggests a mental uneasiness over someone or something in which one has an affectionate interest.
    Solicitude—implies thoughtfulness, often excessive apprehension, for the welfare, safety or comfort of another.
    Worry—suggests mental distress or agitation over some problem.
    Anxiety—suggests an apprehension or uneasy feeling with less mental activity than worry, often over some indefinite but anticipated evil [He viewed the world situation with anxiety.]

    Antonyms: unconcern; indifference[3]

---

[2] John Naisbitt, *Megatrends: Ten New Directions Transforming Our Lives* (New York: Warner Books, 1982), p. 35.

[3] *Webster's New World Dictionary* (2nd College ed.; New York: Simon & Schuster, 1982), p. 214.

The *Reader's Digest Great Encylopedic Dictionary* offers the following definitions:

(1) to have or show regard, interest or concern; (2) to be inclined; (3) to mind or be concerned.
—*to care for:* (1) to look after or provide for; (2) to feel interest concerning; also to have a fondness for; like; (3) want, desire.

Synonyms:
Noun (1) care, concern, solicitude, and worry denote a troubled state of mind. Care arises from responsibility, affection for others, and may vary from mild *concern* to profound *worry*. Concern is the absence of indifference, and hence implies voluntary involvement; concern for the nation's welfare. Solicitude is deep concern arising from kindliness. Worry implies an oppressive and fretful anxiety and is often needless or excessive.

Antonyms:
disregard, indifference[4]

As synonyms for *care, Roget's International Thesaurus* identifies the following verbs: "care, mind, heed—notice, think, consider, take heed or thought of; take an interest, be concerned, be vigilant," as well as "look after" and "take care of." Adjective used in relation to these verbs included "careful, heedful, regardful, mindful, thoughtful, considerate, solicitous, and attentive."[5]

In the nursing literature, the definitions of caring reflect a variety of behaviors. For example, "A simple pat on the back accompanied by a smile can show the patient you care about him as a person."[6] Kohnke states that when a person is in pain or dying, the nurse can respond from four positions of caring. The first two are pity, which is no help, and sympathy, which says the person does not know what to do. The third position is empathy, and Kohnke believes that "this is where most professionals are.... I care and I understand but I can do something for you, and I will because I know how." The fourth position is compassion. "Here you care, here you can act, and from here you can go where that person is."[7] From this fourth position of compassion, one can care to the extent that each human being will allow it.

Carpenito and Duespohl define caring as showing compassion in the

[4] *Reader's Digest Great Encyclopedic Dictionary* (Pleasantville, NY: Reader's Digest Association, 1966), p. 206.

[5] *Roget's International Thesaurus* (3rd ed.; New York: Thomas Y. Crowell Co., 1962), p. 346.

[6] Kathleen McAuliffe, and Delia McAuliffe, "I Care ... Reaching Patients Through Touch," *Nursing '84,* 14, No. 4 (April 1984), pp. 58–59.

[7] Mary Kohnke, "The Nurses's Responsibility to the Consumer," *American Journal of Nursing,* 78, No. 3 (March 1978), p. 441.

client-nurse relationship.[8] They state that caring results when a nurse internalizes feelings of empathy and tenderness. These feelings are reflected actively when one demonstrates true caring in nursing intervention.

Myeroff indicates that caring is the antithesis of using the other person to satisfy one's own needs. He suggests that the meaning of caring should "not be confused with such meanings as wishing well, liking, comforting and maintaining, or simply having an interest in what happens to another."[9]

Travelbee, too, expresses the belief that caring means having compassion for another and communicating the feelings to another.[10] One cannot feign caring, even using elaborate communication techniques. Caring means that the nurse is concerned about the person who is the patient and seeks to intervene in a manner appropriate to alleviate the stress.

Hixon writes that caring is a first-contact communication—letting someone know that one is concerned about him or her as an individual.[11] Caring in nursing involves the transmission of caring in a short time to a stranger. According to Hixon, most nurses do care (are caring) and are concerned.

REVIEW OF LITERATURE

A review of current literature revealed that some concepts are mentioned more frequently than others in the expression of ideas about caring. These concepts are communication, listening, concern, compassion, humanness, support, sharing, empathy, and responsibility.

Leininger has probably been recognized more than any other nurse for her work in identifying caring constructs. Her conceptual and theory-generating model for studying transcultural and enthnonursing constructs identifies 19 major taxonomic caring constructs and segregates.[12] She developed the model in 1968, with revisions and additions in 1972, 1975, and 1976 and continues to be involved in research related to caring.

Leininger stresses the importance of norms, attitudes, and support systems of caring in relation to an individual. These serve as guidelines for tailor-made nursing plans. In addition, she emphasizes the need to derive ideas about *how* caring is viewed, *who* provides the caring, and

[8] Lynda Carpenito and T. Andrea Duespohl, *A Guide for Effective Clinical Instruction* (Wakefield, MA: Nursing Resources, 1981), p. 43.

[9] Milton Myeroff, *On Caring* (New York: Perennial Library, 1971), p. 1.

[10] Joyce Travelbee, *Interpersonal Aspects of Nursing* (Philadelphia: F.A. Davis Co., 1971), p. 143.

[11] J. K. Hixon, "How Can They Tell That We Care?" *AORN Journal*, 39, No. 5 (April 1984), pp. 766–767.

[12] Madeleine Leininger, *Transcultural Nursing: Concepts, Theories, and Practices* (New York: John Wiley and Sons, 1978), p. 39.

under *what* circumstances. Leininger also postulates that individuals who establish a culturally defined caring ritual throughout their lives would demonstrate a better record of stability and maintenance of health than those who have not established such caring rituals.

It seems particularly fitting that a number of authors focus on the elderly when writing about caring. A rapidly changing society with a bent toward high technology provides an excellent environment for increased emphasis on the need for caring. Partridge expresses her ideas about this need in an article concerning nursing values in a changing society. She seems to be saying to nurses that even though we cannot quantify love and caring, they do exist. As she states "... We have all been touched by the serenity, even joy of patients and their families who experienced nursing and health care delivered in warm, caring ways."[13]

But how can patients and their families tell that we care? Hixon is concerned about this and, in her response to her own question, ponders whether we need to relearn that we are in a caring profession.[14] She discusses communication as a means of providing a message of caring, admonishing us to listen to words but also to be aware of other cues, such as tone of voice and speed of speech. Additional communication may be through the eyes. For example, is direct eye contact made? Does the nurse look beyond the patient when talking to him or her? What kind of caring message is sent in this situation? Hixon believes that caring communication takes little time and may prevent misunderstanding. She identifies behaviors such as a pat on the hand, a moment of undivided attention, an explanation of a delay, listening, or sharing a short silence. Verbal and nonverbal communication may convey a message of caring or its antithesis—indifference. However, communication patterns vary and may send different messages of confirmation or disconfirmation to the patient.[15]

Travelbee notes that "it is probably an act of courage to care because in caring one exposes himself to the chance of being hurt by the objects of his care."[16] Although this may occur, the probability of the nurse being hurt by those for whom he or she is caring does not seem great. And, even though the caregiver has needs and rights, it is the patient who is most vulnerable and perhaps most sensitive to caring or indifference.

Ebersole, like Travelbee, believes that one needs courage to care. Courageous caring means freely entering into the pain of others so that

[13] K. B. Partridge, "Nursing Values in a Changing Society," *Nursing Outlook*, 26, No. 6 (June 1978), p. 356.

[14] Hixon, *op. cit.*, p. 766.

[15] Nancy Sharts Engel, "Confirmation and Validation: The Caring that is Professional Nursing," *Image: The Journal of Nursing Scholarship*, 12, No. 3 (October 1980), pp. 53–56.

[16] Travelbee, *op. cit.*, p. 65.

it may be shared. Ebersole emphasizes the need for an in-depth humane approach to caring, based on Christian tenets. His own philosophical stance and religious background as a chaplain in a medical center are reflected in his presentation of ideas. He states:

> ...Caring is not dependent on the conditions of freedom given by others but on the free choice of one who accepts the limitations and brokenness that are written into human existence. It is in that free choosing, to become the one for the others, that freedom becomes a reality. To care at all, requires us to find ourselves by freely entering into the suffering of others.[17]

Jordan's writing about nursing practice emphasizes that caring is synonymous with nursing—caring about and caring for others. This writer interprets his suggestion of sharing to mean that the nurse has the necessary knowledge, skills, attitudes, and perceptions to assist the patient to achieve goals. In Jordan's view:

> Caring for and about each other as nurses is the basic ingredient of caring for and about others. ... Caring includes a caring for ourselves as human beings with dignity, caring for our colleagues, other nurses, and caring for those to whom we offer and provide nursing care. There is nothing new about nursing as caring, but there is evidence that many of us have moved away from caring in the way that I have defined it as the direct care of patients—the laying on of hands.[18]

Myeroff, a noted philosopher, wrote a book entitled *On Caring* in a series on world perspectives.[19] It explores the meaning of caring in a dynamic and highly complex society as perceived by a philosopher. In an epilogue to the volume explaining the meaning of "world perspectives," Anshen wrote:

> It is the thesis of World Perspectives that man is in the process of developing a new consciousness which, in spite of his apparent spiritual and moral captivity, can evenutally lift the human race above and beyond the fear, ignorance, and isolation which beset it today.[20]

Myeroff identifies some major ingredients of caring: knowledge, alternating rhythms, patience, honesty, trust, humility, hope, and courage.

---

[17] Ebersole, *op. cit.*, p. 19

[18] Clifford H. Jordan, "Caring and Sharing: Spectrums of Practice," *AORN Journal*, 38, No. 6 (December 1983), p. 1003.

[19] Myeroff, *op. cit.*

[20] Ruth Anshen, "Epilogue: World Perspectives," in *ibid.*, p. 89.

His ideas concerning knowledge as a base for caring interaction are congruent with what many people regard as the foundation of nursing; namely, that in order to care one must understand another's needs and intervene appropriately in response to those needs. Good intentions do not guarantee this. In caring for someone, a person needs to *know* many things: the strengths and weaknesses of the person receiving help and what his or her needs are, as well as one's own strengths and limitations. Myeroff believes that what we know in caring we know in different ways, both explicitly and implicitly.

Myeroff's concept of alternating rhythms refers to moving back and forth between a narrower and wider framework of reference. This might be analogous to an assessment framework to determine needs. Patience, as an ingredient of caring, means allowing another to grow in his or her own time and own way. It fits with the notion that we actively participate with another to assist in that person's growth to an optimum level of wellness.

Myeroff's view of honesty could be an integral part of any meaningful caring and could serve as a base for nurse-client interaction:

> In caring I am honest in trying to see truly. To care for the other, I must see the other as it is and not as I would like it to be or feel it must be. If I am to help the other to grow, I must respond to its changing needs. If I have to see the other in a certain way, if I can see only what I would like to see, I will not be able to see the other as it really is.[21]

Trust in caring refers to allowing the other person the freedom to grow, avoiding overprotectiveness. A lack of such trust might lead a nurse to make all the decisions for a patient and fail to see the need to assist the person to become more independent. This nurse is not responsive to the patient's needs.

In specifying humility, hope, and courage as ingredients of care, Myeroff indicates a view of the caring person as one who is ready and willing to learn from others and always seeking more knowledge—one who has a sense of the possible and the courage to go into the unknown. This raises the question for nursing of whether we are willing to learn from others who may have less educational preparation but more experience—for example, caregivers of chronically ill patients. If a family is using alternate forms of caring, it may truly lead the nurse into the unknown.

Several writers have suggested that the supportive relationship is essential in caring. Grossman-Shultz and Freeley report on a working model of support. They interviewed 17 nurses working in the Ambulatory Services Department of the Montreal Children's Hospital using a question-

---

[21] Myeroff, *op. cit.*, pp. 18–19.

naire to get these nurses' perceptions of support and their use of supportive behavior. They found:

> For a successful supportive interaction to occur with the client, the nurse's behavior must be governed by: a sense of warmth and genuiness, and a sense of respectfulness for the client, family and their primary concerns. Without these basic tenets, no supportive measure, no matter how appropriate, will be successful.[22]

In writing about the act of caring as expressed in a code of ethics, Roach emphasizes the concept of respect in which the nurse recognizes the specific need for care.[23] The right to self-determination and dignity are integral parts of a framework that embraces caring. A code of ethics enhances the caring person's ability to deal with difficult situations in life. The code of ethics may be the framework that provides guidance for decision making in caring. It may affect the behaviors of caring demonstrated by nurses.

As already noted, empathy is frequently identified in the literature as being related to caring. LaMonica believes that empathy is the primary ingredient in the helping relationship and that it is the helper's responsibility to create a helping relationship which reflects genuineness, warmth, and sensitivity.[24] To be effective in a helping relationship, one must know and understand the other's world. To state it in a different way, one needs to "walk a mile in another's shoes" to have the type of understanding essential in establishing a helping or caring relationship.

Stetler's study on the relationship of perceived empathy to nurses' communication provides a descriptive analysis of verbal and vocal communicative behaviors of nurses. The study involved overall verbal and vocal behaviors of high and low empathizers. Acording to Stetler:

> Verbal, nonverbal, and vocal communication are integral elements within any communication situation; and in all likelihood the key to the perception of empathic understanding does not reside within any one of these channels of communicatoin but within a complex combination of all three with congruency among the three as the factor of primary importance.[25]

The data revealed a significant difference in the communication received by different patients based on certain positive variables: support, pro-

---

[22] Mary Grossman-Shultz and Nancy Freeley, "A Working Model of Support," *The Canadian Nurse*, 80, No. 2 (February 1984), p. 45.

[23] Sister M. Simone Roach, "The Act of Caring as Expressed in a Code of Ethics," *The Canadian Nurse*, 78, No. 6 (June 1982), pp. 30–31.

[24] E. L. LaMonica "Empathy Can Be Learned," *Nurse Educator*, 8, No. 2 (Summer 1983), pp. 19–23.

[25] Cheryl B. Stetler, "Relationship of Perceived Empathy to Nurses' Communication," *Nursing Research* 26, No. 6 (November-December 1977), p. 437.

vision of information requested, and reinforcement.

What about the consumer's point of view? The recipient of caring has a "front-row seat"—a full view of the interaction involved in caring. Jones presents the reactions of one patient who differentiated the type of care offered by first-, second-, and third-year students. The patient described the first-year students as being "at the peak of their compassion, second-year students as more thorough in their work, and third-year students as enrollees who distance themselves from the patient."[26] It is a sad situation that compassion trails off as a student progresses through the educational program. One of the failings of professional nurses as viewed by the patient was their unwillingness to recognize that patients have some knowledge about their bodies and their condition. Jones states that ". . . choosing to keep [the patient] at arm's length gives nurses the upper hand, enabling them to retain that power attendant upon the professional mystique."[27]

This type of behavior is not congruent with Myeroff's view of the caring person who is willing to learn from others. Why are we willing to answer questions from other health professionals who become patients but unwilling to share information with lay persons? If indeed one is manifesting the caring behaviors identified as listening and sharing, why is a line drawn as to what one will listen to and what one will share?

In a study related to patients' reactions to nurses' helping behaviors, Allen, Fraser-Smith, and Gottlieb examined the following questions: (1) To what extent was responsive nursing practiced in three selected settings? (2) Did the health outcomes differ from one setting to the next? and (3) What was the relationship between differences in the type of nursing care provided and the health outcomes of the patients?[28] The authors identified responsive behaviors of nurses and planned their study to describe and demonstrate this type of practice and to evaluate its effectiveness in comparison to assistant-to-the-physician and replacement-of-the-physician versions of the expanded role. They selected three family medicine units in university hospitals for the investigation. They found that nurses in a demonstration setting implemented the critical characteristics of responsive nursing to a greater extent than nurses in the comparison settings.

These researchers described the type of nurse most effective in helping patients deal with stress-related events as one who spends more time with clients or patients, spends little time on clerical tasks, is often available to patients, is a supportive listener, uses time with patients to focus on discussion and listening, and has goals for the clients or pa-

---

[26] Irene Jones, "From a Consumer's Point of View . . . Reactions of One Patient to the Care He Received," *Nursing Times,* 79, No. 31 (August 1983), p. 31.

[27] *Ibid.,* p. 32.

[28] Moyra Allen, Nancy Fraser-Smith, and Louise Gottlieb, "What Makes a Good Nurse?" *The Canadian Nurse,* 78, No. 8 (September 1982), pp. 42–45.

tients. Additional study is needed to evaluate the quality of care administered by a responsive nurse.

In *Perspectives on Clinical Teaching,* Smith briefly discusses compassion, another one of the attributes identified earlier in the definition of caring.[29] She indicates that compassion is the bridge that can carry the nurse's skill and concern to those who need her most.

One of the definitions of caring cited earlier was "take care of"; it seems appropriate, therefore, to look at Wiedenbach's statement concerning the helping art of clinical nursing:

> The helping art of clinical nursing is a deliberate blending of thoughts, feelings and overt actions. It is practiced in relation to an individual who is in need of help, is triggered by a behavioral stimulus from the individual, is rooted in an explicit philosophy and is directed toward fulfillment of a specific purpose.[30]

Weidenbach emphasizes that the patient is vulnerable and presents a need for help. The need for knowledge and the ability to apply the knowledge provides part of the framework for nursing. In the view of this writer, it enhances the ability of the nurse to develop some of the caring attributes described previously. The philosophical stance provides the beacon for coping with the realities of caring. One's philosophy provides not only a foundation that shows whence the person comes, but it also is the means to help project the future.

USES OF THE CONCEPT

The concept of caring can be used in various way. It can be used as the basis for a holistic approach to study humans with biopsychosocial needs. The concepts of knowledge, empathy, support, communication (including listening), responsibility, and sharing provide a conceptual framework for meeting the needs of people in a multicultural, multiethnic, dynamic society.

The concept of caring can also be used to further develop a theoretical foundation in nursing practice. A theory is a group of internally consistent statements that may be used to describe, explain, control, or predict; therefore, the concepts or definitions in this analysis can provide the basis for development of relational statements that provide new insight into the phenomenon of caring. These concepts and definitions can be the source of questions for research findings to increase the knowledge in nursing. A theory-based practice is the goal of research.

---

[29] Dorothy Smith, *Perspectives on Clinical Teaching* (New York: Springer Publishing Co., 1968), p. 8.

[30] Ernestine Wiedenbach, *Clinical Nursing—A Helping Art* (New York: Springer Publishing Co., 1964), p. 11.

The concepts included in the definition of caring could be used to determine standards of care for patients or clients throughout the life span and in highly specialized areas involving high technology. The standards of care could be utilized in developing criteria to evaluate the care.

The review of literature presented here verifies that there are physical as well as psychological and sociological uses for the concept. Caring for a person's physical needs involves knowledge as well as support, communication, sharing, empathy, and responsibility. The same conceptual basis is involved in meeting psychosocial needs.

CRITICAL ATTRIBUTES

Critical attributes related to the concept of caring include the following:

1. There must be interaction between a patient or client and the nurse.
2. There must be some response to the interaction.
3. There must be a need.

Antecedents

Antecedents are those events or incidents that must occur prior to the occurrence of the concept.[31] For caring, they include:

1. Ability to perceive another persons's need.
2. Ability to receive and respond to cues of the persons involved in the caring process.
3. Commitment to sharing with another.

Consequences

Consequences are those events or incidents that occur as a result of the concept.[32] For caring, they include:

1. Increased self-esteem of the client or patient.
2. Increased self-care by patient or client.
3. Improved self-acutalization.
4. Increased exchange of information between nurse and client or patient.
5. More willingness by client to try to reach optimum level of functioning.

---

[31] Lorraine Walker and Kay Avant, *Strategies for Theory Construction in Nursing* (Norfolk, CT: Appleton-Century-Crofts, 1983), p. 33.

[32] *Ibid.*

Model Case Example

This model case reflects the concepts identified in this analysis as part of caring. Mr. J. was 86 years of age when he was admitted to a nursing home because his physical disabilities made it impossible for his wife to care for him. He had arthritis, which had affected his knees, fingers, and shoulder joints, as well as congestive heart failure. He had recently had a transurethral resection and had a resulting problem of dribbling and incontinence.

The nurse who was assigned to care for Mr. J. did a complete assessment and ascertained his physical and psychosocial needs. As she helped him with is exercise routine, she talked with him and encouraged him. She worked diligently to keep him clean and dry. She listened to him when he talked about how it felt to be physically dependent on someone else. She assured him that she enjoyed working with him and was pleased with his efforts to reach the goals that they established together. She worked with him at a pace that would accommodate his needs. She let him know that she could imagine how painful his swollen joints must be. She encouraged his wife and friends to visit him. She never left her tour of duty without going to his room to tell him goodbye and indicating that she would return the next day or telling him the date for her next tour of duty.

Negative Case Example

The following case is an example in which the concept of caring was not applied. A 90-year-old man was admitted to the hospital for a tranurethral resection. The nurse came to hs room to take his vital signs, but did not talk to him while collecting these data. The procedure was implemented correctly but without comment. The patient's wife was in the room, but the nurse was too busy to talk with her. The nurse explained the consent form, inquired if there were any questions, and asked the patient to sign it.

The Challenge of Caring

The concept of caring is complex, and caring confronts an individual with the deeper meanings of his or her life. It offers a challenge to anyone involved in planning for human needs on an individualized basis. Nursing works best when nurses are willing to share and care.

HIGH TECHNOLOGY
AND THE ELDERLY:
A MIXED BLESSING?

SISTER MARY ANNE MULLIGAN, OP, EdD
Director, Certificate Program in Gerontology
Ohio Dominican College
Columbus, Ohio

Our technological world seems to be calling into question the value and worth of every human being. Is it surprising, then, that elderly people, products of an industrialized culture, may be viewed as dependent and nonproductive members of the oncoming electronic world?

Given the sparsity of research on how high technology is affecting the older population, I have dared to ask the question, "Is high technology a mixed blessing for the elderly?" This, in turn, led to two more questions: "What are the attitudes of the elderly toward technical innovation?" and "If the value of the human person is being questioned, how safe is the older population in an ageist society?" This paper will not attempt to solve the problems raised by these questions. Rather, I hope to make those of us who are concerned about the possibility of humanistic concerns being subordinated to high technology more aware of the facts connected with the problems facing us in our care of the elderly.

Because of the broadness and complexity of high technology and the diversity of the needs of our older generation, the paper has necessarily been limited in scope. Technology will be discussed primarily in terms of the health care field; and the elderly's acceptance of and rejection by high technology in a society tainted with ageism will be explored. The question, "Is high technology a mixed blessing for the elderly?" will be answered in the affirmative. Older people's appreciation of the blessings resulting from the use of technological advances will be contrasted to the abuse that results if high technology *alone* is the goal of our scientific achievements. Naisbitt says it better when he advises that our technological society must "balance the material wonders of technology with the spiritual demands of our human nature."[1]

ATTITUDES TOWARD HIGH TECH

Bruce Merrifield, Assistant Secretary of Commerce, predicted that there would be more technological change in the next 10 to 20 years than has happened in all history.[2] How will older people react to the fulfillment of this prophetic statement?

It would seem that the older generation, having lived through many radical changes in their lifetime, are not alien to changes brought about by technological concepts. They have lived from the horse-and-buggy days to the Space Age, when men and women are studying the elements in outer space, their voices echoing back to earth through the vastness. Older people are also aware that some of the most exciting strides in technology are associated with the space program. Spinoffs of space technology, targeted to health problems in later life, are on the increase. Heart problems, for example, are being helped by the implantable defibrillator, a device to monitor electrocardiograms continuously. Biotelemetry units, which monitor the vital functions of astronauts, are now being modified by the development of cassette recorders to monitor electrocardiogram wave lengths. Reliable and rechargeable pacemakers that remove the risk of complications arising from repeated surgery are also a product of National Aeronautics and Space Administration (NASA) ingenuity.[3]

Other parts of the human body will also benefit from space technology. A "mitt" will be on the market to be used as an exercise device. This will help to restore the fingers of an arthritic patient or normal functioning of the hand to burn or stroke victims. A pain reliever called a "human tissue stimulator" will allow the physician to program treatment according to the individual's need.[4] All these technological devices (cost notwithstanding) either are available now or will be in the near future.

What older person would not appreciate technology that provides ways of becoming more medically self-reliant and more responsible for one's

---

[1] John Naisbitt, *Megatrends: Ten New Directions Transforming Our Lives* (New York: Warner Books, 1982), p. 36.

[2] Quoted in Monroe Karmin, et al., "High Tech: Blessing or Curse?" *U.S. News & World Report*, January 16, 1984, p. 36.

[3] June B. Faris, "Technology Promises Increased Convenience and Challenges to the Nation's Elderly," *Aging* (May-June 1983), pp. 12–17.

[4] *Ibid.*, p. 15.

own health? The older generation count among their blessings computers that play the role of healer in the patient's own home. The victim of hypertension, for instance, has two instruments of great help. A hand-held computer (selling for 50 dollars) will measure stress and help with relaxation techniques. A home blood pressure device will allow the hypertensive person, who must keep track of blood pressure measurement daily, the ability to do so accurately.[5]

There seems to be no limit to the technological possibilities of making up for the limitations accompanying the aging process. At the recent National Research Conference on Technology and Aging, supported by the U.S. Department of Health and Human Services Administration on Aging, forecasts were made of technological developments that, without doubt, will have a positive effect on our aging population. The elderly can expect more healthful years in which to have quality as well as quantity of life if technological advances, such as the following, become a reality:

> increased medical uses of computers within health facilities and the home;
>
> replaced parts to produce artificial sight, speech, and hearing, and to carry out body functions formerly performed by now damaged organs;
>
> new computer information systems, which link home telephone service, the TV set and a service network, that permit emergency medical advice in situations of incapacitation or severe trauma;
>
> devices to solve the many problems arising from memory loss in the older adult.[6]

Nor should nursing home residents be overlooked in exploring attitudes of the elderly toward high technology. One study found that nursing home residents do "savor a new kind of 'Apple' "—an Apple computer, that is. Having seen young people on television enjoying video games, a group of nursing home patients needed little persuasion to take part in a study to determine what enjoyment they would get if computer games were made available to them. The findings are worth noting because they indicate the positive effects that computers had on the participants of the study:

> Having access to computers made the sample of 35 residents feel they were "a part of the age of technology." . . . A sizeable number of the sample had relatives working with compuers, and residents were anxious to tell them of their experience.[7]

[5] Kevin Anderson, "Computers and You: Life in the Information Age," *Sky* (June 1984), p. 26.

[6] Elias Cohn, ed., *Newer Markets—Older People* (Washington, D.C. and San Francisco, CA: Gerontological Society of America and Western Gerontological Society, n.d.).

[7] "Nursing Home Residents Savor a New Kind of 'Apple,'" *Aging* (November-December 1982), pp. 29–30.

The experience, they said, "cleared the rust out of the brains." The staff as well as the residents themselves expressed surprise a the residents' capacity to concentrate and to coordinate hand and eye. One of the most constructive findings, which could promote a positive attitude toward high technology among the institutionalized aged, was the improvement in their self-image. Nursing home residents, for the most part, are aware that "society, the institution, even family and friends see them on an irreversible, downhill course which will end in senility and physical deterioration."[8] This study proved otherwise.

Technological forcasting gives promise of books on microchips, games linked by telecommunication channels, and the expansion of television capacity to 300 or more channels—all of which suggests new leisure time activities, particularly for impaired mobile people in nursing homes and in the community.[9]

Another study to determine the attitude of older people toward technology was made by the American Association of Retired Persons in 1981 and 1983. A national telephone survey of 1,308 members confirmed the hypothesis that older individuals have a high degree of interest in new technologies, especially if they are personally useful to them.[10]

HIGH-TECH ADVOCATES FOR THE ELDERLY

There is little doubt that the moral support of key people, who speak in support of continued technological advances to benefit homebound and institutionalized aged, influences attitudes and perceptions of older people toward technology. Cyril F. Brickfield, Executive Director of the American Association of Retired Persons, did this at a symposium on Aging and Technical Advances in 1983. He urged not the rejection of technology, but rather the harnessing of its forces for the benefit of humanity.[11] Brickfield spoke in the interest of the increasing number of older people receiving medical treatment in their own homes who are in need of "high-tech" equipment.

At a Special Committee Hearing on Aging in May 1984, Representative Edward Roybal, Chairman of the House Select Committee on Aging, encouraged more technical advances for the use of communty-based elderly. He told witnesses at the hearing:

Technology has the potential to improve all aspects of the lives of older people. It can enchance their employment, educational and

---

[8] *Ibid.*, p. 30.

[9] Cohn, ed., *op. cit.*

[10] "Elderly Embrace New Technologies," *Modern Maturity* (October-November 1984), p. 17.

[11] Cyril F. Brickfield, "Attitudes and Perceptions; of Older People Toward Technology: The Human Element," *Vital Speeches*, 49, No. 23 (September 15, 1983), pp. 721-724.

recreational opportunities, while assisting them to function independently within their own homes and communities.[12]

In summary, although the information is sparse, there is reason to believe that the elderly, judged on age alone, are not adverse to technological advances. But their interest lies not in high technology for its own sake, but rather in high technology for the sake of the people. These people, however, are victimized by the national prejudice called "ageism." It may be that this type of discrimination is partly responsible for the negative attitude of the elderly toward high technology in medical health care today.

MEDICINE, AGEISM, AND TECHNOLOGY

Ageism, a bias of our youth-oriented and industrialized society, will die hard as long as younger generations see older people as different from themselves and do not identify with them as human beings. According to Butler, who coined the term, "Ageism is a systematic sterotyping of and discrimination against people because they are old, just as racism and sexism accomplish this in relation to skin color and gender."[13]

The most deleterious effect of ageism is the loss of the uniqueness of the person as a human being. Elderly people are people like everyone else. They are in senescence, a developmental stage of their later years. If we live long enough, all of us, without exception, will note a loss of vitality and an increase of vulnerability due to the biological process of aging. Aging is not a disease but a normal process. Disease, however, can hasten aging.

Lawton claims that nowhere is the attitude against aging more manifest than among the health professionals.[14] As he notes, however, it is well known that the medical and allied health training institutions, from which these professionals come have yet to recognize medical gerontology or geriatrics as a specialty. Moreover, medical professionals are products of an "ageist" society, with its multitude of negative cultural attitudes toward the elderly.[15] Fortunately, as Lawton notes, medical institutions are beginning to provide appropriate training in geriatrics. This should bring about a better understanding of the vicissitudes of aging on the part of those who practice health care.

---

[12] "Elderly Embrace New Technologies," p. 17.

[13] Robert N. Butler and Myrna I. Lewis, *Aging and Mental Health* (St. Louis, MO: C.V. Mosby Co., 1977), p. ix.

[14] Alfred H. Lawton, "Issues for Medical Care Personnel," in W. E. Winston and A. E. Wilson, eds., *Ethical Considerations in Long Term Care* (St. Petersburgh, FL: Eckerd College Gerontology Center), 1977, p. 150.

[15] Butler and Lewis, *op. cit.,* p. 142.

I have only admiration for the nursing personnel I have witnessed who recognize their patients as unique individuals with human needs. The regard these nurses have for the worth of their elderly patients, their innate dignity, and their right to be treated as adults is evident.

All too often, however, nurses in hospitals where high technology has been introduced into an intensive care unit (ICU) find that the technology helps them care *for* but not *with* their patients and families. They witness

> the family spending long hours as if in limbo waiting; they are waiting for the latest report, for all too few and brief times when they can see the patient, and for the even fewer times when they see the doctor. . . . They sit in silence, isolated and all but ignored.[16]

Nurses are doing something about this situation. In some hospitals programs have been designed to give the families and patients every opportunity to ease their anxieties and concerns.[17] Channels are provided for the physician and ICU nursing staff to give families relevant information concerning the patient in ICU. Families in waiting rooms are encouraged to share common concerns with other families.

Worthington de Toleda has written about the importance of giving priority to caring *for* an intubated patient before caring *about* the ventilator.[18] Her study showed that an intubated patient, usually critically ill, is subject to increased tension and anxiety due to constant noise, incessant movement, and interruption of sleep, whether in an ICU, a recovery room, or a patient's room. The stress that comes from repeated exposure to this environment can culminate in physical or mental breakdown. Therefore, Worthngton de Toleda advises that the nurse who is alert to alleviating the stress of this situation should make inaudible any equipment that can be safely muffled. It is also important to explain to the patient the medical procedures, which the medical staff take for granted but which may be a source of terror for the patient. Whether the patient is alert or comatose, the nurse is urged to speak to the patient often, orienting him or her to time and place.

Such procedures may be time consuming, but they are very important, especialy to the older person who may be subject to reality disorientation. In fact, attempts to safely help the patient minimize the fears resulting from high-tech equipment may be among the most important efforts that can be made in the patient's behalf.

There is reason to believe that humanistic nursing care will be sorely tested by the ever-increasing intricacies of high technology in health care

---

[16] Nancy J. Chandler, "How to Make a Lonely Place A Little Less Lonely," *Nursing '82* (October 19, 1982), p. 48.

[17] *Ibid.*

[18] Laura Worthington de Toleda, "Caring for the Patient—Instead of the Ventilator: Priorities that Keep the Machine in Its Place," *RN* (Debember 1980), pp. 20-23.

facilities. Recently the *Citizen,* a newspaper in Ottawa, Ontario, Canada, carried the headline, "Scientists Developing Robots to Perform Nursing Duties." The article reported that James McEwen, director of biomedical engineering at Vancouver General Hospital, is currently working on three robot designs, one of which is an "operation room nurse" capable of passing scapels and other instruments to the doctor.[19] However, McEwen's claim that robots would "maintain the quality of diagnosis and treatment is without foundation. Aside from the impersonal environment created by this "nurse-substitute," what can a robot do if the patient, regardless of age, needs some life-saving measure?

The health profession, as one of the last bulwarks of a humane society, has a greater obligation than ever before in the history of medicine to protect the inherent value and dignity of every human being, even those not wanted or valued by others.[20] This is no small task in a technological society that does not hesitate to overlook the rights of human beings in an effort to ensure scientific progress. However, the medical professions are not alone in their effort to maintain the utmost respect for human life. They will find a "humanitarian high tech" in the works of several contemporary authors.

Toffler, for example, writes in *The Third Wave* that there is a rebellion by people against the ever-increasing pace of technology. He claims that there is "a fast growing army of people who are not necessarily anti-technological but who see in the uncontrolled technological thrust a threat to themselves and to global survival.[21] Ellul has this to say about technology as a means and people as an end:

> We should by no means conclude that man is mechanized and conditioned, that he is a robot. . . . Man is still perfectly capable of choosing, deciding, altering, directing, but always within the technological framework and toward the progression of technology.[22]

Naisbitt believes that people are tending toward a highly personal value system to compensate for the impersonal nature of technology. He claims that the medical care field exemplifies his formula for response to technology: "high tech/high touch."[23]

In summary, it can be said that the existing and potential advances of high technology are a mixed blessing for the aging population. There is little doubt that technological advances have arrested diseases and

---

[19] Cited in "Robot Nurse?" *Nursing '84* (December 1984), p. 62.

[20] Joseph L. Bernadine, "Personalist Humanism: Value System for Medicine," *Hospital Progress,* 72 (March 1980), pp. 48–51.

[21] Alvin Toffler, *The Third Wave* (New York: William Morrow & Co. 1980), p. 166.

[22] Jacques Ellul, *The Technological System* (New York: Continuum Publishing Corp., 1980), p. 325.

[23] Naisbitt, *op. cit.,* pp. 36, 39.

disabilities of old age and allowed an extension of the years of relative independence for the aged. This, as well as many other advantages of living in a technological society, contributes to the positive attitude of the elderly toward high technology. On the other hand, in an ageist and industrial society, the older population has cause for fear if their value as human beings becomes secondary to the advances of high technology.

Research is needed on the role that high technology will continue to play in the medical care field. The impersonal nature of technology requires an in-depth study of how people, especially older people, are being affected by the rapidly changing technological advances. The medical profession can play a significant role in preserving humanitarianism in the high-tech world of the future.

PART 3:
RESEARCH
IN LONG-TERM CARE

GERONTOLOGICAL NURSING RESEARCH: 1975 TO 1984

IRENE BURNSIDE, RN, MS, FAAN
Associate Professor, Gerontological Nursing
San Jose State University
San Jose, California

This discussion of the state of the art of gerontological nursing is divided into five parts: (1) analyses of four previous overviews of gerontological nursing, (2) findings of a survey of gerontological research from 1975 to 1984, (3) current trends in gerontological nursing research, (4) unstudied phenomena and needed research, and (5) application of studies or concepts from other disciplines.

GERONTOLOGICAL NURSING OVERVIEWS

Three overviews of gerontological nursing research by Gunter and Miller, Robinson, and Kayser-Jones and one overview on gerontological nursing literature by Basson provided background for this paper.[1] Basson's survey covered an 11-year review of articles published in gerontological nursing. Canadian and United Kingdom journals were included in the review, so it was an expansive undertaking. Gunter and Miller, Robinson, and Kayser-Jones limited their searches to the United States. However, Gunter and Miller and Robinson do mention the work of

---

[1] L. M. Gunter and J. C. Miller, "Toward a Nursing Gerontology, *Nursing Research,* 26 (1977), pp. 208–221; L. Robinson, "Gerontological Nursing Research," in I. Burnside, ed., *Nursing and the Aged* (2nd ed.; New York: McGraw-Hill Book Co., 1981), pp. 654–666; J. Kayser-Jones, "Gerontological Nursing Research Revisited," *Journal of Gerontological Nursing,* 1 (1981), pp. 217–223; and P. H. Basson, "The Gerontological Nursing Literature Search: Study and Results," *Nursing Research,* 16 (1967), pp. 267–272. Kerr's overview on theory and research related to use of space in hospitals did not focus on the elderly; it is recommended, however, because of the section on implications for research, which bears on the care of the elderly in acute settings. *See* J. A. C. Kerr, "An Overview of Theory and Research Related to Space Use in Hospitals," *Western Journal of Nursing Research,* 4 (1982), pp. 395–405.

Doreen Norton, who has long been a pioneer in geriatric nursing research in Great Britain.[2] Gunter and Miller, Robinson, and Kayser-Jones also included non-nursing journals in their reviews, in contrast to the present survey, which tapped only nursing journals.

Basson

Although Basson's overview did not focus only on research, the survey is important because it was the first major effort, published in 1967, to describe the state of the art in gerontological nursing.

A limitation of the overview was the lack of a reference list of articles and studies analyzed. A large portion of the content of the article was devoted to the logistics of the search itself. That early review also noted a selective emphasis on two diseases; cardiovascular accidents and arteriosclerosis constituted over half of the coverage.

An important finding of the review was the great lack of research emanating from a theoretical stance or reflecting a theoretical framework. Basson noted: "Instead there is an overwhelming emphasis on information needed to solve a particular problem. Needed are efforts directed towards devloping generalizations which can be applied to a range of problems."[3] Although there was an increase in research and empirical studies in the late 1960s, the paucity of theoretical development continued throughout the period of the study. A total of 52 research articles were published; 34 empirical studies were tallied in the survey.

Over 300 of the 438 references identified in the survey were concerned with meeting the psychosocial needs of the patients. Regarding education, there were few articles on gerontological nursing education. Articles about in-staff education and speciaized programs (Basson did not define what specialized programs were) had the highest frequencies; only one article about graduate education was reported.

Gunter and Miller

A decade later, Gunter and Miller analyzed studies published in *Nursing Research* from 1952 to 1976. They stated that gerontological nursing research reflected minimal attention to the integration of biological, psychological, and sociological knowledge. They also urged that caution be exercised when theory from other disciplines was applied to nursing phenomena. The authors noted that nursing investigators did not study the promotion of mental health or preventable aspects of mental disabilities that are common in later life. They concluded that no research being done at that time utilized a nursing theoretical framework.

[2] D. Norton, R. McLaren, and A. N. Exton-Smith, *An Investigation of Geriatric Nursing Problems in Hospital* (London: Churchill Livingston, 1976; originally published by the National Corporation for the Care of Old People, 1962).

[3] Basson, *op. cit.*, p. 272.

Gunter and Miller stated that the need for more nursing research in psychosocial nursing was critical. There were apparent delays in applying what was already known about the elderly to nursing care. There was also evidence that insufficient numbers of nurses were well prepared as researchers at the doctoral level.

Robinson

Robinson conducted a systematic review of gerontological nursing research and, as Basson had noted 14 years earlier, observed that "... the vast majority of the research has been reported without reference to an underlying theoretical framework."[4] The frameworks that did provide the underpinnings of studies were drawn from a wide range of theoretical or conceptual bases. Only a few studies were based on physical science theory; the majority of the studies incorporated frameworks from behavioral or social science theories.

Specific studies bearing on education for gerontological nursing were closely related to studies on attitudes. Robinson found no studies that addressed undergraduate issues in gerontological nursing education. Robinson stated that new knowledge gained had to be disseminated to geriatric nurse practitioners, educators, and researchers.

Kayser-Jones

Kayser-Jones originally presented her research overview at the Second National Symposium on Aging in 1981. In contrast to Gunter and Miller, who analyzed only *Nursing Research,* Kayser-Jones surveyed four nursing journals: *Geriatric Nursing, Journal of Gerontological Nursing, Research in Nursing and Health,* and *Western Journal of Nursing Research.* These journals were surveyed from the beginning of publication through July 1980. *Nursing Research* was surveyed from January 1977 to July 1980. The author located 44 research articles. Table 1 lists the focus of the research articles surveyed.

Like the researchers before her, Kayser-Jones noted that past research had focused on the psychosocial needs of the institutionalized aged. Few clinical studies handled the prevailing problems of drug interactions and constipation. Kayser-Jones noted the need for more clinical studies on incontinence, confusion, immobility, and use of sedative-hypnotic drugs. Her recommendations also included longitudinal studies, stimulating research in gerontological nursing, increased research to investigate mental health care needs of the aged, and availability and use of community mental health centers.

---

[4] Robinson, *op. cit.*, p. 656.

Table 1. Focus of Research Articles Surveyed by Kayser-Jones*

Focus	Number
Clinical focus	12
Psychosocial problems	9
Attitudes	7
Institutionalized elderly	7
Health needs of elderly in community	3
Sexuality	2
Minority	2
Gerontological nursing research reviews	2

* J. Kayser-Jones. "Gerontological Nursing Research Revisited." *Journal of Gerontological Nursing.* 1 (1981), pp. 217–223.

Highlights of the Overviews

A few similiarities may be noted in these overviews. All the authors discussed the fascination of nurse researchers with the topic of attitudes. Basson, in fact, found that "of the 174 mentions of nurse-patient interactions, 40.8 percent were on some aspect of nursing staff attitudes toward the patient."[5] Robinson found 8 studies that focused on attitudes; Gunter and Miller documented 7 studies; Kayser-Jones also found 7. The present review located 21 such studies, which may indicate either that the obsession is on the increase or that more editors are interested in publishing reports on that topic. In fact, the entire October 1982 issue of the *Journal of Gerontological Nursing* was devoted to an "in-depth focus on attitudes about aging." *Nursing Research,* the oldest nursing journal devoted exclusively to research, has published 9 studies on attitudes. As Smith states, "The researcher decides a priori the subject matter sought by delineating the dilemma situations of nurses, patients, or nurses and patients."[6] The dilemma situation focused on continues to be the attitudes of nurses or student nurses.[7] Other studies on attitudes conducted by nurses were found in journals not included in the current survey, so actually the total number of available articles in the ten-year period of the study exceeds 21.

[5] Basson, *op. cit.*

[6] M. C. Smith, "Research Methodology: Epistemologic Considerations," *Image: The Journal of Nursing Scholarship,* 16 (1984), p. 45.

[7] The seminal work of De Lora and Moses on students' attitudes is widely quoted. *See* J. R. De Lora and D. V. Moses, "Specialty Preference and Characteristics of Nursing Students in Baccalaureate Programs," *Nursing Research,* 18 (1969), pp. 137–144. Fifteen years later, in a study of student nurses, De Lora found that although there was a drop in student nurses' listing of geriatrics as the least preferred of the specialties, there was an increase in descriptions of it as "depressing" and "boring." De Lora, unpublished research data, Department of Sociology, San Diego State University, San Diego, CA., 1984, Tables C, D, and E.

Another important finding in the surveys of Basson, Gunter and Miller, and Robinson, but not confirmed in the present one, was a lack of theoretical frameworks. An additional common finding was the lack of studies on effective educational programs at all levels. Robinson, as well as Gunter and Miller, clearly enunicate the need for doctorally prepared nurses. Kayser-Jones elaborated on the inadequate pool of candidates for doctoral study, many of whom may enter with insufficient preparation. Moreover, the lack of qualified faculty members requires students to compensate for their deficiencies. Basson and Robinson both pointed out that the early writings were informational, anecdotal, and geared toward solving problems.

A SURVEY OF GERONTOLOGICAL
NURSING RESEARCH: 1975-1984

Because of the tremendous increase in gerontological nursing research in the United States, a fifth overview is timely. A survey was made of four selected journals from January 1975 through December 1984. These journals—*Journal of Gerontological Nursing, Research in Nursing and Health, Western Journal of Research,* and *Nursing Research*—were hand searched for studies about older subjects. These journals were selected because they consistently published most of the research on aging done the past decade.

No books, chapters, or conference papers were included in the search, and only research conducted by nurses was included. If the first author of a multiple-authored study was not a nurse, the study was omitted. Research was included if a sample of subjects was specified as "geriatric age" or if the specified age, mean, or median in the sample description identified subjects as being over 60 years of age. Occasionally, reseachers did not state the age of subjects. If the sample was composed entirely of nursing home residents, the study was also included because they were likely to be elderly.

Four types of studies, some of which did not have elderly subjects, were also included: (1) studies on delivery of services, (2) attitude studies, (3) studies that used incident reports as data, and (4) research on developing instruments. None of the studies listed were evaluated. Although the importance and contributions of master's and doctoral studies cannot be ignored, none were included in this survey because they are less accessible than the journals.

Table 2 summarizes the gerontological nursing research during the last decade. As already noted, attitudes continue to be a favorite focus of gerontological nursing research. Studies examined the attitudes of

Table 2. Studies by Gerontological Nurse Researchers, 1975 to 1984

Category	Number
Nursing activities	23
Attitudes	21
Drugs	8
Curriculum, gerontological nursing and knowledge	7
Delivery of service	6
Accidents and falls	6
Behaviors	5
Health needs/practices	5
Instruments and tools	5
Time perception	4
Mental status, morale, satisfaction	4
Locus of control	4
Relocation	3
Territoriality, personal space	3
Life change events	2
Sleep	2
Disengagement	2
Bereavement, loneliness	2
Sexuality	1
Total	
	113

student nurses,[8] nursing care providers,[9] health professionals,[10] the elderly,[11] and adolescents.[12] There is also a report of a simulation game on attitudes toward aging.[13] Studies on attitudes are also widely scattered in other journals.[14]

Much current research is based on "popular" concepts, for example, disengagement,[15] locus of control, life change events, relocation

[8] G. Chamberland et al., "Improving Students' Attitudes Toward Aging," *Journal of Gerontological Nursing,* 4 (1978), pp. 44–45; S. P. Damrosch, "Nursing Students' Attitudes Toward Sexually Active Older Persons," *Nursing Research,* 31 (1982), pp. 252–255; J. Hannon, "Effect of a Course on Aging in a Graduate Nursing Curriculum: A Small Descriptive Study," *Journal of Gerontological Nursing,* 6 (1980), pp. 604–614; L. K. Hart, M. I. Freel, and C. M. Crowell, "Changing Attitudes Toward the Aged and Interest in Caring for the Aged, *Journal of Gerontological Nursing,* 2 (1976), pp. 11–16; J. S. Kayser-Schmit and F. A. Minnigrode, "Increasing Nursing Student Interest in Working with Aged Patients," *Nursing Research,* 24 (1975), pp. 23–26; S. S. Robb, "Attitudes and Intentions of Baccalaureate Nursing Students Toward the Elderly," *Nursing Research,* 28 (1979), pp. 43–50; M. J. Roberts and C. Powell, "The Rape of Geriatrics by Fundamental Nursing Instructors," *Journal of Gerontological Nursing,* 4 (1978), pp. 35–37; K. H. Taylor and T. L. Harned, "Attitudes Toward Old People: A Study of Nurses Who Care for the Elderly," *Journal of Gerontological Nursing,* 4 (1978), pp. 43–47; and M. J. Wilhite and D. M. Johnson, "Changes in Nursing Students' Stereotypic Attitudes Toward Old People," *Nursing Research,* 25 (1976), pp. 430–432.

[9] H. T. Brower, "Social Organization and Nurses' Attitudes Toward the Aged," *Journal of Gerontological Nursing,* 1 (1981), pp. 294–298; B. A. Devine, "Old Age Stereotyping: A Comparison of Staff Attitudes Toward the Aged," *Journal of Gerontological Nursing,* 6 (1980), pp. 25-31; M. Futrell and W. Jones, "Attitudes of Physicians, Nurses, and Social Workers Toward the Elderly and Health Maintenance Services for the Aged: Implications for Health Manpower Policy," *Journal of Gerontological Nursing,* 3 (1977), pp. 42–46; J. Hatton, "Nurses' Attitude Toward The Aged: Relationship to Nursing Care," *Journal of Gerontological Nursing,* 3 (1977), pp.21–30; L. C. Mullins and S. Merrian, "Nurses React to Death Anxiety," *Journal of Gerontological Nursing,* 9 (1983), pp. 487–492; and T. S. Tharp, B. S. Baker, and T. F. Brower, "Nursing Staff Attitudes Toward Geriatric Nurse Practitioners," *Nursing Research,* 28 (1979), pp. 299–301.

[10] C. A. Dye, "Attitude Change Among Health Professionals: Implications for Gerontological Nursing," *Journal of Gerontological Nursing,* 5 (1979), pp. 31–35; and S. M. Tollett and C. M. Adamson, "The Need for Gerontologic Content within Nursing Curriculum and Other Conclusions Based on a Recent Survey," *Journal of Gernontological Nursing,* 8 (1982), pp. 576–580.

[11] B. A. Devine, "Attitudes of the Elderly Toward Religion," *Journal of Gerontological Nursing,* 6 (1980), pp. 679–685; and S. J. Tobiason et al., "Positive Attitudes Toward Aging: The Aged Teach the Young," *Journal of Gerontological Nursing,* 5 (1979), pp. 18–23.

[12] J. A. Hernan, "Effect of Gerontological Educational Experience on Adolescent Girls' Attitudes Toward the Elderly," *Journal of Gerontological Nursing,* 7 (1981), pp. 45–49.

[13] G. M. Chaisson, "Life-Cycle: A Social-Stimulation Game to Improve Attitudes and Responses to the Elderly," *Journal of Gerontological Nursing,* 6 (1980), pp. 587–592.

[14] M. M. Meyer, R. S. Hassanein, and R. T. Bahr, "A Comparision of Attitudes Toward the Aged Held by Professional Nurses," *Image: The Journal of Nursing Scholarship,* 12 (1980), pp. 62–66; and B. R. Heller, and F. R. Walsh, "Changing Nursing Students' Attitudes Toward the Aged: An Experimental Study," *Journal of Nursing Education,* 15 (1976), pp. 9–17.

[15] B. S. Henthorn, "Disengagement and Reinforcement in the Elderly," *Research in Nursing and Health,* 2 (1979), pp. 1–8; and J. O. Edsell and L. A. Miller, "Relationship Between Loss of Auditory and Visual Acuity and Social Disengagement in an Aged Population," *Nursing Research,* 27 (1978), pp. 296–302.

effects,[16] time perception,[17] and reality orientation as a treatment modality.[18] In general, there appears to be an appropriate use of theories selected from other disciplines.

Accidents and falls pose dilemmas for both the nurse and the patient. All the studies on this topic used incident reports to study accidents and falls.[19] No observational studies of elderly individuals studied behavior prior to a fall or behaviors that might indicate who is at high risk for a fall.

The following phenomenon were subsumed under the broad category of nursing activities: body temperature,[20] care plan entries,[21] constipation,[22] confusional states,[23] exercise,[24] feeding,[25] movement,[26]

[16] L. M. Simms, S. J. Jones, and K. Yoder, "Adjustment of Older Persons in Nursing Homes," *Journal of Gerontological Nursing*, 8 (1982), pp. 383-386; and C. Grey, "Moving 137 Elderly Residents to a New Facilitity," *Journal of Gerontological Nursing*, 4 (1978), pp. 34-42.

[17] K. D. Melillo, "Informal Activity Involvement and the Perceived Rate of Time Passage for an Older Institutional Population," *Journal of Gerontological Nursing*, 6 (1980), pp. 392-397; M. A. Newman, "Time as an Index of Expanding Consciousness with Age," *Nursing Research*, 31 (1982), pp. 290-293; and Newman and J. K. Gaudiano, "Depression as an Explanation for Decreased Subjective Time in the Elderly," *Nursing Research*, 83 (1984), pp. 137-139.

[18] M. Hogstel, "Use of Reality Orientation with Aging Confused Patients," *Nursing Research*, 28 (1979), pp. 161-165; V. L. Nodhturft and N. M. Sweeney, "Reality Orientation for the Institutionalized Elderly," *Journal of Gerontological Nursing*, 8 (July 1982), pp. 396-401; H. Settle, "A Pilot Study in Reality Oreintation for the Confused Elderly," *Journal of Gerontological Nursing*, 1 (1975), pp. 11-16; and D. Voelkel, "A Study in Reality Orientation and Resocialization Groups with Confused Elderly," *Journal of Gerontological Nursing*, 4 (1978), pp. 13-18.

[19] M. J. Kustaborder and M. Rigney, "Interventions for Safety," *Journal of Gerontological Nursing*, 9 (1983), pp. 159-162; E. G. Barbieri, "Patient Falls Are Not Patient Accidents," *Journal of Gerontological Nursing*, 3 (March 1983), pp. 164-173; J. Colling and D. Park, "Home, Safe Home," *Journal of Gerontological Nursing*, 9 (1983), pp. 175-183; R. R. Feist, "Survey of Accidental Falls in a Small Home for the Aged," *Journal of Gerontological Nursing*, 4 (1978), pp. 15-17; G. Gould, "A Survey of Incident Reports," *Journal of Gerontological Nursing*, 1 (September-October 1975), pp. 23-26; and M. Louis, "Falls and Their Causes," *Journal of Gerontological Nursing*, 9 (1983), pp. 142-149.

[20] R. Thatcher, "98.6F—What is Normal?" *Journal of Gerontological Nursing*, 9 (1983), pp. 22-27.

[21] E. A. Hefferin and R. E. Hunter, "Nursing Observation and Care Planning for the Hospitalized Aged," *Gerontologist*, 15 (1975), pp. 57-60.

[22] E. G. Battle and C. E. Hanna, "Evaluation of a Dietary Regimen for Chronic Constipation: Report of a Pilot Study," *Journal of Gerontological Nursing*, 6 (1980), pp. 527-532; and C. Wichita, "Treating and Preventing Constipation in Nursing Home Residents," *Journal of Gerontological Nursing*, 3 (1977), pp. 35-39.

[23] M. A. Williams et al., "Nursing Activities and Acute Confusional States in Elderly Hip-Fractured Patients," *Nursing Research*, 28 (1979), pp. 25-35.

[24] C. A. Karl, "The Effect of an Exercise Program on Self-Care Activities for the Institutionalized Elderly," *Journal of Gerontology*, 8 (1982), pp. 282-285; and C. J. Parent and A. J. Whall, "Are Physical Activity, Self-Esteem and Depression Related?" *Journal of Gerontological Nursing*, 10 (1984), pp. 8-11.

[25] M. M. Baltes and M. B. Zerbe, "Reestablishing Self-Feeding in a Nursing Home Resident," *Nursing Research*, 25 (1976), pp. 24-26.

[26] W. G. Goldberg and J. J. Fitzpatrick, "Effect of Movement Therapy Group on Morale and Self-Esteem," *Nursing Research*, 29, No. 6 (1980), pp. 339-346; and B. L. Roberts and J. J. Fitzpatrick, "Improving Balance--Therapy of Movement," *Journal of Gerontological Nursing*, 9 (1983), pp. 150-155.

oral history,[27] oral hygiene,[28] positioning,[29] reality orientation,[30] touch,[31] treating hands of cerebrovascular accident patients,[32] urinary incontinence,[33] range of motion,[34] and treatment of dysphagia.[35] The guideline for inclusion in this category was that the researcher had intervened in a condition. Although other studies surveyed described phenomena that might require nursing intervention, the researcher may not have chosen to study the results of intervening. For example, the response of patients to a transfer was the problem in one study, but the author did not study intervention or what was done to prevent or alleviate translocation trauma.[36] It should be noted that many of these appear to be independent studies; few are replications. The lack of repeated findings in studies of phenomena makes it difficult for nurses to make decisions based on sound research. However, the scope of phenomena to be studied is awesome. The lack of studies on other phenomena regarding the aged will be discussed later.

Nursing activities and attitudes comprised 44 of the 113 studies. Drugs were the focus of eight studies,[37] and seven examined curriculum or

[27] E. M. Donahue, "Preserving History Through Oral Reflections," *Journal of Gerontological Nursing,* 8 (1982), pp. 272–278.

[28] E. M. DeWalt, "Effect of Time Hygienic Measures on Oral Mucosa in a Group of Elderly Subjects," *Nursing Research,* 24 (1975), pp. 104–108.

[29] K. Lamb, "Effect of Positioning of Postoperative Fractured-Hip Patients as Related to Comfort," *Nursing Research,* 28 (September-October 1979), pp. 291–294.

[30] Nodhturft and Sweeney, *op. cit.;* Hogstel, *op. cit.;* Settle, *op. cit.;* and Voelkel, *op. cit.*

[31] R. M. Langland and C. Panicucci, "Effects of Touch on Communication with Elderly Confused Clients," *Journal of Gerontological Nursing,* 8 (1982), pp. 152–155; and L. E. Copstead, "Effects of Touch on Self-Appraisal and Interaction Appraisal for Permanently Institutionalized Older Adults," *Journal of Gerontological Nursing,* 6 (1980), pp. 747–752.

[32] S. Jamison and N. Dayhoff, "A Hard Hand-Positioning Device to Decrease Risk of Finger Hypertonicity: A Sensiomotor Approach for the Patient with Non-Progressive Brain Damage," *Nursing Research,* 29 (1980), pp. 285–289.

[33] K. Dufault, "Urinary Incontinence: United States and British Nursing Perspectives," *Journal of Gerontological Nursing,* 4 (1978), pp. 28–33.

[34] D. H. Clough and J. T. Maurin, "ROM Versus NRx," *Journal of Gerontological Nursing,* 9, No. 5 (May 1983), pp. 278–286.

[35] H. Williams et al., "Treating Dysphagia," *Journal of Gerontological Nursing,* 9 (1983), pp. 638–647.

[36] M. C. Smith, "Patient Responses to Being Transferred During Hospitalization," *Nursing Research,* 25 (1976), pp. 192–200.

[37] M. M. Brown et al., "Drug-Drug Interactions among Residents in Homes for the Elderly," *Nursing Research,* 26 (1977), pp. 47–52; B. S. Fahey and M. R. Grier, "Analgesic Medication for Elderly People Post-Surgery," *Nursing Research,* 33 (1984), pp. 369–372; M. H. Foxall, "Elderly Patients At Risk of Potential Drug Interactions in Long-Term Care," *Western Journal of Nursing Research,* 4 (Spring 1982), pp. 133–146; R. M. Gerber and S. R. Van Ort, "Topical Application of Insulation in Decubitus Ulcers," *Nursing Research,* 28 (1979), pp. 16–19; K. K. Kim and M. R. Grier, "Pacing Effects of Medication Instruction for the Elderly," *Journal of Gerontological Nursing,* 7 (1981), pp. 464–468; S. S. Dittmar and T. Dulski, "Early Evening Administration of Sleep Medication to the Hospitalized Aged: A Consideration in Rehabilitation," *Nursing Research,* 26 (1977), pp. 299–303; C. H. Requarth, "Medication Usage and Interaction in the Long-Term Care Elderly," *Journal of Gerontological Nursing,* 5 (1979), p. 33; and S. Van Ort and R. M. Gerber, "Topical Application of Insulin in the Treatment of Decubitus Ulcers: A Pilot Study," *Nursing Research,* 25 (1976), pp. 9–12.

knowledge base in gerontological nursing.[38] Two new areas of research not noted in the previous overviews are locus of control[39] and time perception.[40]

Health needs of the elderly were studied predominantly by means of survey designs.[41] Two descriptive studies focused on blood pressure readings in ambulatory elderly individuals and the health needs of senior citizens living in high-rise apartments.[42]

The focuses of studies about behavior ranged from confused behavior to nocturnal behavior.[43] Two studies focused on effects of the environment on behavior,[44] and an interesting study by Rosendahl and Ross considered the attending behavior of nurses and how it affected the

[38] J. Baldini, "Knowledge about Hypertension in Affected Elderly Persons," *Journal of Gerontological Nursing,* 1 (1981), pp. 543-551; H. T. Brower, "A Study of Graduate Programs in Gerontological Nursing," *Journal of Gerontological Nursing,* 3 (1977), pp. 40-46; Brower, "A Study of Content Needs in Graduate Gerontological Nursing Curriculum," *Journal of Gerontological Nursing,* 5 (1979), pp. 21-28; J. A. Farrady, "Inservice Training in Extended Care Facilities: A Pilot Project," *Journal of Gerontological Nursing,* 6 (1980), pp. 40-42; A. A. Huckstadt, "Do Nurses Know Enough About Gerontology? Research for a Knowledge Base," *Journal of Gerontological Nursing,* 9 (1983), pp. 392-396; P. A. King and M. Cobb, "Learning to Care," *Journal of Gerontological Nursing,* 9 (1983), pp. 288-292; and S. S. Robb and M. Malinzak, "Knowledge Levels of Personnel in Gerontological Nursing," *Journal of Gerontological Nursing,* 7 (1981), pp. 153-158.

[39] Some of Chang's research on this topic is categorized under instruments and mental status and morale in the table. B. L. Chang, "Perceived Situational Control of Daily Activities: A New Tool," *Research in Nursing and Health,* 1 (1978), pp. 181-188; Chang, "Generalized Expectancy, Situation Perception, and Morale among Institutionalized Elderly," *Nursing Research,* 27 (1978), pp. 316-324; Chang, "Black and White Elderly: Morale and Perception of Control," *Western Journal of Nursing Research,* 2 (1980), pp. 371-385; J. M. Pohl and S. S. Fuller, "Perceived Choice, Social Interaction, and Dimensions of Morale of Residents in a Home for the Aged," *Research in Nursing and Health,* 3 (1980), pp. 147-157; M. B. Ryden, "Morale and Perceived Control in Institutional Elderly," *Nursing Research,* 33 (1984), pp. 130-136; and M. Smallegan, "Decision Making for Nursing Home Admission: A Preliminary Study," *Journal of Gerontological Nursing,* 1 (1975), pp. 11-16.

[40] J. J. Fitzpatrick and M. J. Donovan, "Temporal Experience and Motor Behavior among the Aging," *Research in Nursing and Health,* 1 (1978), pp. 60-68; Melillo, *op. cit.;* Newman, *op. cit.;* and Newman and Gaudiano, *op. cit.*

[41] P. Franck, "A Survey of Health Needs of Older Adults in Northwest Johnson County, Iowa," *Nursing Research,* 28 (1979), pp. 360-364; M. J. Schank and P. Conrad, " A Survey of the Well-Elderly: Their Foot Problems, Practices and Needs," *Journal of Gerontological Nursing,* 3 (1977), pp. 10-15; and S. L. Miller, A. A. Tedford, and S. P. Lehmann, "Identification of Health Problems at Well Elderly Clinics," *Journal of Gerontological Nursing,* 7 (1981), pp. 159-168.

[42] R. T. Bahr and L. Gress, "Blood Pressure Readings and Selected Parameter Relationships on an Elderly Ambulatory Population," *Journal of Gerontological Nursing,* 8 (1982), pp. 159-163; and M. J. Hain and S. P. C. Chen, "Health Needs of the Elderly," *Nursing Research,* 25 (1976), pp. 433-439.

[43] S. E. Chisholm et al., "Prevalence of Confusion in Elderly Hospitalized Patients," *Journal of Gerontological Nursing,* 8 (1982), pp. 87-96; and L. D. Gress, R. T. Bahr, and R. S. Hassanein, "Nocturnal Behavior of Selected Institutionalized Adults," *Journal of Gerontological Nursing,* 7 (1981), pp. 86-92.

[44] P. B. Lester and M. M. Baltes, "Functional Interdependence of the Social Environment and the Behavior of the Institutionalized Aged," *Journal of Gerontological Nursing,* 4 (1978), pp. 23-27; and S. S. Robb, M. Boyd, and C. Pristash, "A Wine Bottle, Plant and Puppy: Catalysts for Social Behavior," *Journal of Gerontological Nursing,* 6 (1980), pp. 721-728.

patients' responses.[45]

Studies on delivery of service covered the range from education and screening for foot problems to measurement of effectiveness of care delivered by community health nurses.[46] Hubbard, Muhlenkamp, and Brown studied social supports and self-care; home care by families was studied by Worcester and Quayhagen; and criteria for quality care in long-term care was the focus of a study by Kayser-Jones.[47]

Current gerontological nursing research also focuses on the development of instruments and tools. Fitzpatrick and Donovan studied the reliability and validity of the motor activity rating scale; Chang designed a measurement of perceived control of situations in daily activities of the institutionalized elderly; Friedman designed a sexual knowledge inventory for older people; King developed an instrument to assess the lower extremities in the aged; and Fulmer and Cahill created an instrument to assess abuse of the elderly.[48]

Mental status, morale, and satisfaction were studied by several researchers. Roslaniec and Fitzpatrick studied mental changes in elderly patients during the first four days of hospitalization.[49] Morale among low-income blacks was the subject of a study by Gilson and Coats.[50] Life satisfaction and morale in institutionalized elderly were also studied.[51] Disengagement, a once popular theory, was studied by Edsell and Miller and by Henthorn.[52]

[45] P. P. Rosendahl and V. Ross, "Does Your Behavior Affect Your Patient's Response?" *Journal of Gerontological Nursing,* 8 (1982), pp. 572–575.

[46] D. Conrad, "Foot Education and Screening Programs for the Elderly," *Journal of Gerontological Nursing,* 3 (1977), pp. 11 ff; J. A. Sullivan and F. Armignacco, "Effectiveness of a Comprehensive Health Program for the Well-Elderly by Community Health Nurses," *Nursing Research,* 28 (1979), pp. 70–75; and J. Thornbury and A. Martin, "Do Nurses Make a Difference?" *Journal of Gerontological Nursing,* 9 (1983), pp. 440–445.

[47] P. Hubbard, A. F. Muhlenkamp, and N. Brown, "The Relationship between Social Support and Self-Care Practices," *Nursing Research,* 33 (1984), pp. 266–269; M. I. Worcester and M. P. Quayhagen, "Correlates of Care Giving Satisfaction: Prerequisites to Elder Home Care," *Research in Nursing and Health,* 6 (1983), pp. 61–67; and J. Kayser-Jones, "Care of the Institutionalized Aged in Scotland and the United States: A Comparative Study," *Western Journal of Nursing Research,* 1 (1979), pp. 190–200.

[48] J. J. Fitzpatrick and M. J. Donovan, "A Follow-up Study of the Reliability and Validity of the Motor Activity Rating Scale," *Nursing Research,* 28 (1979), pp. 179–181; Chang, "Perceived Situational Control of Daily Activities"; J. S. Friedman, "Development of a Sexual Knowledge Inventory for Elderly Persons," *Nursing Research,* 28 (1979), pp. 372–374; P. A. King, "Foot Assessment of the Elderly," *Journal of Gerontological Nursing,* 4 (1978), pp. 47–52; and T. Fulmer and V. Cahill, "Assessing Elder Abuse: A Study," *Journal of Gerontological Nursing,* 12 (December 1984), pp. 16–20.

[49] A. Roselaniec and J. J. Fitzpatrick, "Changes in Mental Status in Older Adults with Four Days of Hospitalization," *Research in Nursing and Health,* 2 (1979), pp. 177–187.

[50] P. Gilson and S. Coats, "A Study of Morale in Low Income Blacks," *Journal of Gerontological Nursing,* 6 (1980), pp. 385–388.

[51] Chang, "Generalized Expectancy, Situation Perception, and Morale among Institutionalized Aged"; P. Miller and D. A. Russell, "Elements Promoting Satisfaction as Identified by Residents in the Nursing Home," *Journal of Gerontological Nursing,* 6 (1980), pp. 121–129.

[52] Edsell and Miller, *op. cit.;* and Henthorn, *op. cit.*

Territoriality and personal space has been of interest to nurses for some time, but it is now being researched using the aged as subjects. Personal space of elders was studied by Gioiella and Louis, while living arrangements for elders was the subject of research by Grier.[53]

Studies of sleep that were not focused on interventions were done by Pacini and Fitzpatrick and by Hayter.[54] The former contrasted sleep of hospitalized and nonhospitalized elders. Hayter studied sleep behaviors of older people of various ages, an indication that nurse researchers are no longer lumping subjects into the "60 and older" category.

Relocation was studied by three researchers. Grey was interested in mortality rates after relocation; Simms, Jones and Yoder studied residents' adjustment to the nursing home; and Smith studied responses of patients to transfer within the hospital.[55]

The study of life change events was the focus of two studies. Muhlenkamp, Gress, and Flood studied perception of life change events by the elderly, and Fuller and Larson studied social supports that enhance the older person's ability to cope with life events.[56]

Widowhood, secondary loneliness, and the effects of a sexuality class for elders each constituted topics for a single research study during this period.[57]

TRENDS IN GERONTOLOGICAL NURSING RESEARCH

As gerontological nursing research moves forward, changes and trends are emerging. A notable change compared to trends found by previous overviews is the inclusion of a variety of theoretical frameworks as the base for research by nurses. Collaborative efforts have also increased. There are more experimental designs; tighter controls are in place; more sophisticated statistical data analyses are made, and computerized data is widely used.

---

[53] E. C. Gioella, "The Relationships between Slowness of Response, State Anxiety, Social Isolation and Self-Esteem, and Preferred Personal Space in the Elderly," *Journal of Gerontological Nursing,* 4 (1978), pp. 40-43; M. Louis, "Personal Space Boundary of Elders: An Empirical Study," *Journal of Gerontological Nursing,* 7 (July 1981), pp. 395-400; and M. R. Grier, "Living Arrangements for the Elderly," *Journal of Gerontological Nursing,* 3 (1977), pp. 19-22.

[54] C. M. Pacini and J. J. Fitzpatrick, "Sleep Patterns of Hospitalized and Non-Hospitalized Aged Individuals," *Journal of Gerontological Nursing,* 8 (1982), pp. 327-332; and J. Hayter, "Sleep Behaviors of Older Persons," *Nursing Research,* 32 (1983), pp. 242-246.

[55] Grey, *op. cit.;* Simms, Jones, and Yoder, *op. cit.;* and Smith, *op. cit.*

[56] A. F. Muhlenkamp, L. A. Gress, and M. Flood, "Perception of Life Change Events by the Elderly," *Nursing Research,* 24 (1975), pp. 109-113; and S. S. Fuller and S. B. Larsen, "Life Events, Emotional Support, and Health of Older People," *Research in Nursing and Health,* 3 (1980), pp. 81-87.

[57] B. G. Valanis and R. Yeaworth, "Ratings of Physical and Mental Health in Older Bereaved," *Research in Nursing and Health,* 5 (1982), pp. 137-146; G. Francis and S. H. Odell, "Long-Term Residence and Loneliness: Myth or Reality?" *Journal of Gerontological Nursing,* 5 (1979), pp. 9-11; and H. T. Brower and L. S. Tanner, "A Study of Older Adults Attending a Program on Human Sexuality: A Pilot Study," *Nursing Research,* 28 (1979), pp. 36-39.

There are ongoing research efforts, and clusters of studies on a particular phenomenon can be located. Interest in refining or designing instruments and tools is increasing. Innovative demonstration projects have increased sharply.

A particular interest in psychosocial nursing research continues from its early beginning in 1952. One example is the study of reality orientation as a treatment modality. Nurses have pioneered group work with the elderly but now the research, often experimental in design is appearing in the literature. Studies about mental health problems are beginning to surface, and fertile new areas for research are emerging: time perception, locus of control, territoriality, intrusion, privacy, personal space, movement, life change events, bereavement, and animal-human bonds[58] to name a few.

Much of the research reported from 1975 to 1985 was done on a captive audience—nursing home residents. While this choice of subjects reduces generalizability, the importance of improving care for this segment of the population of the aged cannot be overlooked. In a nationwide study of the priorities that nursing needs to address, third on the list of the 15 priorities with the greatest potential for an impact on patient welfare was "Find means of enhancing the quality of life for the aged in the institutions."[59] In the current survey, out of 113 studies, 37 studies selected extended care or intermediate care residents as subjects; incident reports in nursing homes accounted for data in 6 studies.

Individual researchers in gerontological nursing have become known for their expertise in specialized areas; for example, Brower's steady research on gerontological nursing curriculum and attitudes; Chang's studies on locus of control; Fitzpatrick's focus on motor activity; Kayser-Jones's field studies of nursing homes; Newman's research on time perspective; Robb's studies on attitudes on wandering and animal-human bonds; and Wolanin's pioneering taxonomy of confusion and studies on relocation trauma. Although research by Wells and Brink did not appear in this survey, their work on incontinence is well known to nurse gerontologists.[60]

---

[58] L. K. Bustad and L. M. Hines, "Placement of Animals with the Elderly: Benefits and Strategies," *California Veterinarian*, 8 (1982), pp. 37–43.

[59] C. Lindeman, "Delphi Survey of Priorities in Clinical Nursing Research," *Nursing Research*, 24 (1975), pp. 434–441.

[60] Chang, "Perceived Situational Control of Daily Activities"; Chang, "Generalized Expectancy, Situation Perception, and Morale among Institutionalized Aged"; Chang, "Black and White Elderly: Morale and Perception of Control"; Fitzpatrick and Donovan, *op. cit.;* Kayser-Jones, "Care of the Institutionalized Aged"; Newman, *op. cit.;* Newman and Gaudiano, *op. cit.;* Robb and Malinzak, *op. cit.;* Robb, *op. cit.;* M. O. Wolanin and L. Phillips, *Confusion: Prevention and Treatment* (St. Louis, MO: C. V. Mosby, Co., 1981); and T. Wells and C. Brink, "Urinary Continence: Assessment and Managment," in I. M. Burnside, ed., *Nursing and the Aged* (New York: McGraw-Hill Book Co., 1981), pp. 519–548.

UNSTUDIED PHENOMENA AND NEEDED RESEARCH

Based on the analyses of the three overviews described earlier, the gaps found in the survey of research from 1975 to 1985, and the writer's clinical experience, the following lacunae still exist in gerontological nursing research:

Abuse
Alzheimer's disease and care
Catastrophic reactions
Confidants
Cost-effective deliveries
    or therapies
Delirium and dementia
Depression
Exercise and mobility
Health centers for elderly,
    nurse-managed
Hearing problems
Hypothermia and hyperthermia
Incontinence
Infection control

Intensive Care Unit syndrome
Life review therapy
Living arrangements
Nutrition
Paranoia
Pet therapy
Reminiscence therapy
Restraints
Self-esteem
Sensory deprivation or overload
Significant others
Suicide
Sundowner's syndrome
Visual problems
Wandering behavior

Areas in which research is particularly urgently needed to improve quality of care include: abuse, care of Alzheimer's patients and families, day care centers, nurse-managed centers, and cost-effective delivery systems. The important role of nurses as caregivers will become more apparent as significant research results appear in the literature.

The pragmatic, day-to-day problems in long-term care and chronic illness do not have the esoteric appeal that other topics do. Nevertheless, Benedict, a director of a skilled nursing facilities department in a utilization project, has offered a list of suggested evaluation studies.[61] Table 3 presents these practical, nitty-gritty problems in long-term care that are waiting to be researched. The reader should note that few of the topics on the list are psychosocial in nature.

Other writers paint the research needs of gerontological nursing with a wider brush. Knowles, a long-time gerontologist, states:

> Research in geronotological nursing needs to proceed with all possible speed. Health conditions among the elderly, particularly in the chronically ill and disabled categories, and related problems

[61] S. Benedict, "Medical Care Evaluation Studies for Utilization Review in Skilled Nursing Facilities" (Rockville, MD: Social Security Administration, Department of Health, Education and Welfare, 1975).

Table 3. Needed Evaluation Studies of Nursing Home Care

Admission/discharge of residents

1. Direct source of patients (hospital, other skilled nursing facility, home, etc.)
2. Postdischarge destination and use of home care programs
3. Frequency of readmissions within two weeks of discharge
4. Appropriateness of admissions

Responsibilities of nurses and physicians

1. Use of nurses for non-nursing functions
2. Patient charts reflecting "skilled nursing"
3. Appropriateness of visits by attending physicians
4. Timeliness of diagnostic services
5. Incident reports
6. Most common diagnoses and type and amount of skilled services required for treatment

Nursing care

1. Weight loss of patient
2. Effectiveness of bowel and bladder training
3. Need for bowel and bladder training program
4. Care of the dying resident

Drugs

1. Source of drugs and effectiveness of delivery
2. Adequacy of policies and procedures for medications
3. Medications and the diet
4. Drug study (amounts and possible interactions)

Source: S. Benedict, "Medical Care Evaluation Studies for Utilization Review in Skilled Nursing Facilities" (Rockville, MD: Social Security Administration, Department of Health, Education and Welfare, 1975).

of nursing practice are researched by students. The absence of gerontological nurse specialists on their theses or dissertation committees reduce the quality of the students' learning experience [p. 52].[62]

Knowles also points out that the knowledge base is still in the developmental stage and suggests more research based on healthful coping patterns as well as more cost-effectiveness studies are needed.

Harrington and Cruise state that gerontological nursing research should be focused on the long-range goals, such as measuring outcomes of nursing activities. These writers suggest that it is timely to study the power structures within the health care system and how to go about changing the system to improve care for clients. The focus should be on conflict and power. Research, according to Harrington and Cruise, "tends to be specialized and trivialized rather than directed toward major critical economic and political issues."[63]

Abdellah stresses the importance of research in long-term care:

> Particularly needed are special research efforts to design quality assessment tools that will take into account the limited patient outcome goals and complex treatment processes characteristic of much long-term care. Research in this area also needs to be addressed to health financing systems for delivery of services, and methods that provide access to services.[64]

RESEARCH FROM OTHER DISCIPLINES

The delays in applying what is already known about the elderly reaffirms what Gunter and Miller stated in 1977.[65] Findings from other researchers should guide nurses as they move into the special needs of the aged. Some of the subjects of research from other disciplines that could provide the theoretical or conceptual frameworks for nurse researchers include (1) cognitive decline after continued, untreated high blood pressure, (2) relocation trauma and multiple and conflicting findings, (3) the intensive care unit syndrome, (4) the importance of the confidant, (5) the role of pets, (6) reminiscence therapy, (7) life review therapy, (8) the role of nurses as group leaders of the aged, and (9) learning in the elderly.

[62] L. Knowles, "Gerontological Nursing 1982," *International Journal of Nursing Studies*, 20 (1983), p. 52.

[63] C. Harrington and M. Cruise, "Leadership in Gerontological Nursing," *Gerontology and Geriatrics Education*, 4 (1984), p. 109.

[64] F. G. Abdellah, "U.S. Public Health's Contribution to Nursing Research—Past Present Nursing," *Nursing Research*, 26 (1977), p. 247.

[65] Gunter and Miller, *op. cit.*

GENERAL COMMENTS

The lack of adequate definitions of terminology in gerontological nursing research becomes readily apparent in conducting the literature search. As Bloch has described this problem: "A term's definition goes to the heart of the understanding of the concept underlying that term. Such understanding and defining is necessary for adequate operationalization of a concept."[66] Thus, one way to improve the scholarship of current gerontological nursing research and literature about the aged would be a more discrete use of terminology. Several terms are poorly defined, including *wandering, confusion, confused, life review,* and *reminiscence therapy.* Another term commonly misused in the literature is *reality therapy* in lieu of *reality orientation.* Although researchers can operationally define their terms in the body of the paper, the use of ambiguous terms in titles does not move us toward sharpness or precision in language. And that ambiguity bogs down even the most determined researcher. It is distressing to note that sophisticated researchers still use the word *senile* in their writings.

The words *reminiscing* and *life review* are used interchangeably in current gerontology and nursing literature. Although Butler used the terms synonymously in his seminal work,[67] practitioners generally agree that these are two quite separate and distinct modalities, and after reading studies or articles, it is apparent that the modalities being described are not operationally defined.

Descriptive studies are needed to begin to understand some of the phenomena that clinical nurses have observed for some time. There is a need for case studies, replication studies, and more methodological research to provide more accurate and finely tuned measuring tools. No historical study about gerontological nursing was located; this is another rich area for study. Longitudinal studies by nurses would be a giant step forward. Studies from large research projects also need to find their way into the literature.

The crucial need for effective curricula for nurses at all levels mandates increased research. Doctoral students are expected to publish results of their studies. Master's students need to be encouraged to publish findings from their studies as well. More studies on the frail elderly, the very old, are urgent because of the changing demographic patterns.[68] Their special needs are not yet known; perhaps their care will become a specialty all its own.

---

[66] D. Bloch, "Interrelated Issues in Evaluation and Evaluation Research: A Researcher's Perspective," *Nursing Research,* 29, (1980), p. 69.

[67] R. N. Butler, "The Life Review: An Interpretation of Reminiscence in the Aged," *Psychiatry,* 26 (1963), pp. 65–76.

[68] M. Futrell, "Research in Gerontological Nursing," *Journal of Gerontological Nursing,* 6 (1980), p. 515; and Futrell, "Get Involved in Research," *Journal of Gerontological Nursing,* 10 (1984), p. 6.

No nurses in this survey published studies on two conceptual frameworks that are widely cited in geropsychology and geropsychiatry: life review and exclusion of stimuli.[69] There was a glaring lack of research by geropsychiatric nurses.

Another area for future study is personal qualities that might move individuals toward better health or self-actualization. Possibilities include: coherence,[70] hardiness,[71] stability,[72] and hope.[73] All have relevance for study in elderly individuals.

If studies continue to accrue in the literature at the present steady rate, a meta-analysis may soon be appropriate. And, finally, there is a need for research on the quality of care and the quality of life as it is perceived by the elderly.

SUMMARY

This survey covered a ten-year period and included only six of the many nursing journals. Although it was not an exhaustive search, the findings do offer a view of the kaleidoscopic array of phenomena. Progress has been noted. The phenomena nurses have chosen to study indicates their continued concern for the psychosocial aspects of care of the aged, possibly a reflection or an indicator of the great concern for holism in gerontological nursing. Downs asks: "Precisely what is nursing knowledge and what concrete phenomenon, events and processes constitute the bedrock of nursing science?"[74] These questions need to be applied to gerontological nursing research.

Smith states: "The problem of nursing practice resides in the concrete instances of persons in a situation of being nurses and patients. The 'persons' are incalculably complex."[75] The elderly truly are "incalculably complex—individuals fighting for their individuality, coping with multiple diagnoses and multiple losses, and living in the last phase of life—indeed a challenge. And the research to be done on their behalf is also a great challenge for gerontological nurses.

[69] Butler, *op. cit.;* and J. Weinberg, "On Adding Insight to Injury," *Gerontologist,* 16 (1976), pp. 4–10.

[70] A. Antonovsky, *Health, Stress and Coping* (San Francisco: Jossey-Bass, 1979).

[71] S. Kobasa, S. Maddi, and S. Kahn, "Hardiness and Health: A Prospective Study," *Journal of Personality and Social Psychology,* 42 (1982), pp. 168–177.

[72] B. Hall, "Toward an Understanding of Stability in Nursing Phenomena," *Advances in Nursing Science,* 5 (1983), pp. 15–20.

[73] B. J. Limandri et al., "Instilling Hope," *American Journal of Nursing,* 78 (1978), pp. 79–80; R. Lincoln, "What do Nurses Know about Confusion in the Aged?" *Journal of Gerontological Nursing,* 10 (1984), pp. 26–29; R. F. McGee, "Hope: A Factor Influencing Crisis Resolution," *Advances in Nursing Science,* 6 (1984), p. 34; R. T. Roessler et al., "The Paradox of Hope for Individuals with a Disability," *Psychosocial Rehabilitation Journal,* 2 (1978), pp. 1–8; and J. A. Werner-Beland, "Nursing and the Concept of Hope," in Werner-Beland, ed., *Grief Response in Long-Term Illness and Disability* (Reston, VA: Reston Publishing, 1980).

[74] F. Downs, "Dig We Must," Editorial, *Nursing Research,* 33 (1984), p. 254.

[75] Smith, "Research Methodology," p. 43.

BIBLIOGRAPHY

Batey, M. V. "Conceptualization: Knowledge and Logic Guiding Empirical Research," *Nursing Research,* 26 (1977), pp. 324–329.

Birren, J. E. "Nature of Research on Aging." In Birren, ed., *Handbook of Aging and the Individual.* Chicago: University of Chicago Press, 1959.

Brimmer, P. "Past, Present and Future in Gerontological Research." *Journal of Gerontological Nursing,* 5 (November-December 1979), pp. 27–34.

Donley, R. "Why has Nursing been Slow in Developing a Theoretical Base? *Image: The Journal of Nursing Scholarship,* 12 (1980), p. 2.

Fleming, J. W., and J. Hayter. "Reading Research Reports Critically, *Nursing Outlook,* 22 (1974), pp. 172–175.

Gortner, S. R. "Nursing Science in Transition," *Nursing Research,* 29 (1980), pp. 180–183.

Greenhill, E. D. "An Evaluation of Nursing Students' Attitudes and Interests in Working with Older People, *Gerontology and Geriatrics Education,* 4 (1983), pp. 83–88.

Hoyer, W. J., et al. "Research Practice in the Psychology of Aging: A Survey of Research Published in the *Journal of Gerontology* 1975-1982," *Journal of Gerontology,* 39 (1984), pp. 44–48.

Jacox A., and P. Prescott. "Determining a Study's Relevance for Clinical Practice," *American Journal of Nursing,* 78 (1978), pp. 1883–1889.

Lindsay, A. M. "Phenomena and Physiological Variables of Relevance to Nursing: Review of a Decade of Work," Part II, *Western Journal of Nursing Research,* 5 (1983), pp. 40–63.

Mercer, R. T. "Nursing Research: The Bridge to Excellence in Practice," *Image: The Journal of Nursing Scholarship,* 16 (1984), pp. 47–51.

Notter, L. E. "Empirical Research in Nursing," *Nursing Research,* 20, (1971), p. 99.

Oiler, C. "The Phenomenological Approach in Nursing Research," *Nursing Research,* 31 (1982), pp. 178–181.

O'Neill, C., et al. "Utilizing Research in the Placement of the Elderly, *Journal of Gerontological Nursing,* 7 (1981), pp. 99–103.

Paletta, J. L. Nursing Research: An Integral Part of Professional Nursing. *Image: The Journal of Nursing Scholarship,* 12 (1980), pp. 3–6.

Smith, M. C., and D. C. Naftel. Meta-Analysis: A Perspective for Research Synthesis. *Image: The Journal of Nursing Scholarship,* 16 (1984), pp. 9–11.

Stetler, C. B., and G. Marram. "Evaluating Research Findings for Applicability in Practice, *Nursing Outlook,* 24 (1976), pp. 559–563.

APPENDIX

APPENDIX: STUDY QUESTIONS

These study questions have applicability for individuals and groups in education and service settings. Explorations may be undertaken by students and faculty singularly or in concert with staff and administration in service settings. Select groups of questions may provide the foundation for in-service education programs. Many of the questions can be used for in-depth, independent study.

Strategies for Attracting Staff and Faculty in Long-Term Care

1. What are the proper emphases on well elderly and care of sick and institutionalized elderly in basic educational programs?

2. Recruitment and retention of staff are separate issues with different considerations for different types of staff, such as:
   - Nurse practitioners and clinical specialists
   - Staff
   - Administrative staff

   What are your reasons for agreeing or disagreeing?

3. Identify research studies in nursing to improve practice in long-term care settings.

4. What common clinical nursing problems in long-term care need further research?

Commitment to Clinical Excellence in Nursing Homes

1. What feedback do staff need about the outcomes of practice?

2. What relevant content should be included in continuing education programs in long-term care?

3. Can the faculty of gerontological nurse practitioner programs build upon the experiences of other nurse practitioner models?

4. What changes are indicated in educational preparation to foster confidence and esteem in both faculty and students to encourage practice in long-term care?

5. What are the issues involved in establishing collaborative relationships and shared decision making between directors of nursing service and nursing home administrators?

6. What can be done to increase the market demands for employment of geriatric nurse practitioners?

Attitudes Toward the Elderly: Nursing Students' Perspectives

1. What gaps exist between what is taught and what is practiced in gerontological nursing?

2. What are the issues as you perceive them in "care" versus "cure" for the elderly in various age groupings?

3. What educational background and clinical experience are needed to teach gerontological nursing?

4. What are reasons for the limited number of gerontological nurse role models in education and in practice?

5. What are the constraints in the practice setting that influence gerontological nursing?

6. What suggestions do you have for improving the quality and quantity of students' clinical experiences with elderly clients?

7. How can a systematic approach to discharge planning be developed for older clients in a variety of settings?

Environmental Influences that Affect Nursing Home Staff

1. Why are simple, basic nursing skills not applied to the large number of elderly people?

2. How does one assess the leadership capabilities of nurses to manipulate the long-term care environment?

3. What is the impact on geriatric nursing of increased intensity and acuity in patient care services?

4. What is the potential to cost out nursing services as a revenue-producing center in nursing homes?

5. How does a systematic feedback process contribute to the knowledge base and decision making of the nurse?

Knowledge Competencies in Gerontological Nursing

1. What is the nurse's role in assessment and provision of care to elderly clients?

2. How can funds be identified and increased for research in gerontological nursing?

3. What strategies are needed to market new and different achievements in gerontological/geriatric nursing practice?

4. What strategies could be used by schools of nursing to interest more students in gerontological/geriatric nursing practice?

5. What changes in curricula would help to foster nurses' experiences in policy and decision making for geriatric care and services?

6. Differentiate characteristics of the medical model and nursing model in long-term care.

Core Content in Geropsychiatric Nursing

1. What are the common mental health problems of the elderly?

2. What mental health/psychiatric concepts should be integrated into the nursing assessment of the elderly client?

3. Why are so few faculty members in graduate nursing education seeking funds and developing curricula for geropsychiatric nursing?

4. What are the characteristics of older people who are at high risk for mental health problems or disorders?

5. Why is there underutilization of mental health services by practitioners and older individuals?

6. What is the range of accessible and affordable community health resources for older individuals?

7. What are the legal, regulatory, and reimbursement realities that influence nursing practice?

Caring: A Concept Within Nursing

1. What does the concept of "caring" mean to you?

2. What factors may encourage or discourage students' caring abilities?

3. What are the spiritual dimensions of caring?

4. What variety of behaviors are encompassed in the concept of caring?

5. Define the concept of "reciprocal caring."

6. How can nursing students and personnel be helped to identify and understand reciprocal caring as it pertains to elderly individuals?

High Technology and the Elderly: A Mixed Blessing

1. What does the aging process mean to you?

2. How does "high tech/high touch" relate to aging clients?

3. What is the societal value of the individual in determining the priorities and use of scarce resources?

4. What are the ethical issues regarding decisions about life and death affecting elderly persons?

5. How can medicine and nursing work together on the ethical issues of high technology?

6. What are the effects of ageism on research, education, and service?

Gerontological Nursing Research: 1975 to 1984

1. What available research in gerontology is relevant to nursing practice?

2. Why is it important to replicate selected studies in long-term care?

3. How are the outcomes of the Teaching Nursing Home Project important to gerontological nursing?

4. Why are studies lacking on effective educational preparation of gerontological nurses at all levels?

5. What strategies could be initiated to increase the number of doctorally prepared nurses to carry out geriatric/gerontological research?